GOD IS GREEN, FOR V.
ON EARTH WOULD CEASE TO EXIST

This Garden Earth

By

Peter F. Perry

Illustrated by Perri

This Garden Earth

©Peter F. Perry
Illustrated by Perri

ISBN 1 903607 62 0

Published by Able Publishing 2005

Typesetting and production by:
Able Publishing
13 Station Road
Knebworth
Hertfordshire SG3 6AP

Tel: (01438) 813416 / 812320
Fax: (01438) 815232
Email: books@ablepublishing.co.uk

ABOUT THE AUTHOR

Peter F Perry has been an environmentalist for over forty years. He has written horticultural and environmental articles for such journals as *Gardeners Chronicle, Garden News, The Hardy Plant Society, The National Auricula and Primula Society, The Countryman, Hertfordshire Countryside* and *The Best of British*.

He has also produced numerous drawings for these journals under the name of Perri, and caused quite a sensation in the sixties when he produced a series of front cover designs for *Gardeners Chronicle*, pushing the art of scraper-board to new heights. He is also the illustrator for *this* work.

He has worked on The Hertfordshire County Council *Structure Plan,* The Bedfordshire *Greenspace Action programme,* Stevenage's *Agenda 21, The Real World Alliance, The National Forest project,* the Department of Transport's *Integrated Transport Policy,* and The HGAC & HFEA consultation document, *Cloning issues in reproduction, science and medicine.*

His tireless efforts for wildlife conservation has brought him praise from such well-known figures as Sir David Attenborough, Dr. David Bellamy, and the late Geoff Hamilton.

As a teenager living in London during the era of the *killer smog*, he told his contemporaries that it was not only *smoke from coal fires* that was the killer, as the government of the day were advised, but the *invisible fumes from motor vehicles*.

His elders laughed at him at the time, but, more than thirty years later, in 1991, scientists at Warren Spring laboratories in Stevenage, Herts., discovered *'an invisible killer smog, caused by the reaction of sunlight on petrol fumes'*. This has since become officially recognised as 'ozone smog'.

Since then, Pete has predicted, in his articles, the hole in the ozone layer, global warming, the possibility of astronauts bringing extra-terrestrial disease back from space, and the connection between CJD and BSE, long before they were 'officially' discovered.

For this reason, more and more people are heeding Peter's warnings.

Although his main interests concern the environment, Peter has also has success in *other* fields.

In 1968, his first novel, *Pass me a codeine* was published under the pseudonym *Perry Peterson*. It was a humorous book, based upon Pete's career as a nursing attendant in the R.A.F.

His first *children's* novel, *Tales of Widgeripoo,* was first published by Hamilton & Co. in April 1999, under the name of Pete Perry, and was republished in 2004 by Central Publishing, together with the follow-up, *Tales of Widgeripoo Too.*

Throughout all of Peter's work, however, even in his children's stories, there is a social and environmental theme.

Peter believes that nobody is too young to learn about the values of life, for the future of our planet is the future inheritance of our children.

Website:
http:www.geocities.com/widgeripoo

CONTENTS

An example of a scraper-board illustration by PERRI

PRIMARY INTRODUCTION

How much do we really *understand* plants? Certainly a lot less than we understand *animal* life. Yet if it were not for plants, life on Earth wouldn't even *exist*!

Many people think that plants are merely 'things which grow in the ground to supply us with food, medicine and pleasure'.

In actual fact, plants are a life unto themselves, and they may well understand *us* more than we understand *them*!

It is almost certain that plants were the first life—form to inhabit the Earth. It is certainly a fact that we, and all other animal life would perish without them.

This is not only due to their food and medicinal values, but also because they produce most of the vital oxygen we all need to breathe!

Without plants, all other forms of life on Earth would literally suffocate.

I have been trying to get this point across to the general public, in magazine and newspaper articles, and by word of mouth, since I was a teenager in the fifties. Until The eighties however, when the hole in the ozone layer was discovered, I was regarded as something of an eccentric.

Now I am advising government-sponsored environmental groups on the best way to plan for the new millennium.

This book, which was originally written in 1975 and discarded by publishers as 'too alarmist' or 'too fanciful', begins with a story, based on my own experience. This in turn, leads into the main substance of the book.

From here on, it is split into three parts, *THE STORY OF PLANT LIFE, TIPPING THE SCALES,* and *PLANTS MAY NOT LAUGH OR CRY, BUT THEY'RE SO SENSITIVE!*

We start from the beginning of life itself, tracing the evolution of plant life.

After explaining how Man started off by working *with* nature, we go to explain how he started to *destroy* it through greed and thoughtlessness.

Next, we will go into the *movements* and *sensitivity* of plants. The wonderful devices they have evolved for the purpose of survival and reproduction. we look at some incredible experiments with plants, which indicate that plants not only have *feelings and emotions*, but how they may even be capable of *telepathy*, using *our* senses to enable them to 'see', 'hear', 'smell' and 'taste'!

Finally in our conclusion, we take a trip into the future and try to predict, not only what plant life may be like in the distant future, but what lessons we may learn about plant life, and consequently life *itself*, from the planets in our Solar system and beyond!

By understanding plants, we are a step nearer to understanding life itself.

REMEMBER *GOD IS GREEN, FOR WITHOUT PLANT LIFE, LIFE ON EARTH WOULD CEASE TO EXIST!*

Now let us explore, from the beginning of time, *THIS GARDEN, EARTH ...*

PETER F. PERRY
Environmental Social Journalist
Stevenage, Herts,
U.K.

THE ESSENCE OF LIFE

An introductory story

Les

Frank

'What makes you think you're so different from these Arum lilies?' I asked my mate Les, as we walked through my garden.

'Oh come *off* it Pete!' He retorted. 'For a *start*, I can *move around* wherever I wish, I can *converse with my fellows*, and above all, I have the ability to *think* and *reason!*'

'Are you *sure* about that Les?' Asked my other mate Frank sarcastically.

Frank and I had both worked in horticulture, whereas Les had been in engineering for most of his life. We had all known each other for years, but whereas Frank and I could look beyond the obvious, Les was inclined to be very materialistic.

I smiled at Les's sensitive expression at Frank's remark.

'So you don't think plants *have* these abilities?' I asked Les.

'Of *course* not.' He replied, as though it were a personal affront. 'Plants don't *question* life as *we* do!'

'How do you *know?*' I asked him. 'Have you ever *asked* them?'

'Oh, don't be *stupid* Pete! 'He huffed. 'I can't communicate with a *plant!*'

'I'm not being *stupid.*' I reasoned. 'How can you expect to *communicate* with a plant if you don't *TRY?'*

'That's ridiculous!' He retorted as he relit his pipe for the third time in as many minutes. 'You won't catch *me* making a fool of myself by trying to talk to plants, even if *YOU* do!'

This really *amused* me. Here was my old friend Les, a very successful engineer, but with a mind so narrow as to think that communication between plants and humans is *impossible*. Why, even *Prince Charles* has admitted to talking to plants. Les however, was far too *'practical'* for such flippancies!'

'Do you think, Les,' Asked Frank, 'that there is really so much *difference* between you and a *plant?'*

'Now look here Frank,' he retorted, 'are you insinuating that I'm no better than a *cabbage?'* He relit his pipe again, re-asserted himself and added, 'I haven't noticed any thriving businesses springing up from the *cabbage patch* lately!'

I had to laugh at this comment. After all, *we* are the ones who *complicate* our lives, with worrying about material possessions! A *cabbage*, on the other hand, is quite content with it's lot.

I led Les into my office, which I also use as a small laboratory. I made my way to the microscope.

'Take a look in here,' I invited him, much to Frank's amusement, 'and tell me what you *see …'*

Les peered into the eyepiece.

'Very interesting.' He replied, 'It's a *seed* of some sort, with the outer cover removed …'

'That's right,' I agreed, 'but take a closer look. You'll see that the cotyledons and plumule, that is the seed *leaf* and seed *root,* are all fitted snugly together into the testa, the *seed covering.* The baby plant is all curled up ready for the moment of germination, or *birth!'*

'Well, that *is* interesting.' He muttered. 'I didn't realise that there was actually a *baby plant* curled up in every *seed!'*

'You hit it right on the head, Les,' I emphasized, 'a *BABY* plant, all curled up inside the shell of the seed! It's just like a baby *chick* inside an *egg,* or a *human* baby in it's mother's *womb. NOW* do you see how similar plant and animal life are, at least at the *beginning of life?*'

'Well, yes, *but* …' He stammered.

Frank grinned to himself. He was *enjoying* this!

'Now have a look at this …' I interrupted him.

I put another slide under the microscope.

'A *tissue* of some sort.' He observed as he peered into the eyepiece. 'I remember this from *school biology*. It's a tissue of skin from an *animal* of some sort …'

'No, Les,' I corrected him. 'Oh, it's a *living tissue* all right, but *this* was actually taken from a *lupin plant!*'

'*INCREDIBLE!*' He gasped.

'Not *really*,' I told him. 'It's quite *obvious* when you *think* about it. You see, all life comes from the *same original source!*'

'It just goes to *show* you Les,' Frank joined in, '*You* are made up of the same material as a *lupin!*'

'OK, OK!' He replied grudgingly. 'I'll *grant* you *that!* You can't convince me though, that plants can *think and reason* the way *we* do!'

I didn't reply. Instead, I took him in to the greenhouse, where I pointed out a plant which was growing in sphagnum moss

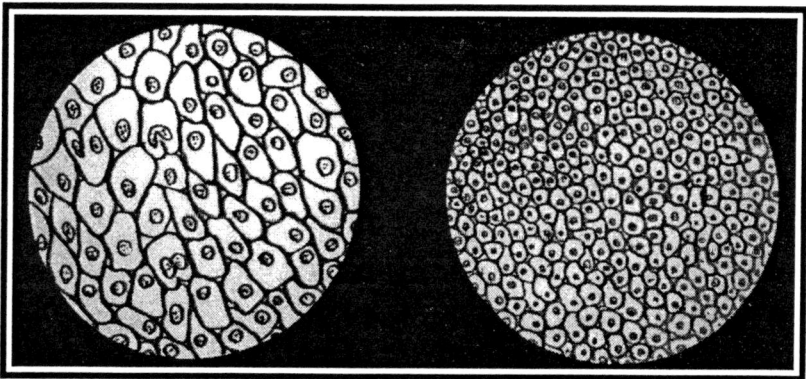

Human tissue   Plant Tissue

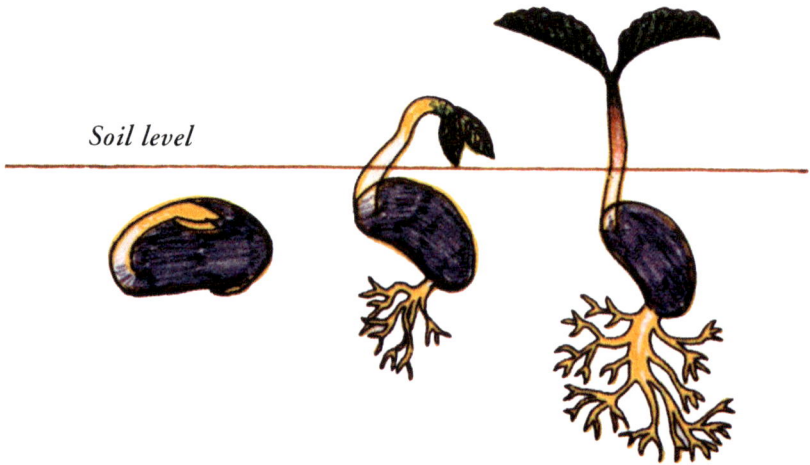

Germination of a seed, showing "curled up" embryo, similar to a chick in the egg, or a baby in the womb.

Venus Fly Trap

'This,' I told him, 'is *Dionea muscipula*, the Venus's Fly Trap...'

'Oh yes, I've *heard* of that.' He said. 'It's one of those things that eat *flies* ...'

'Well, it doesn't actually eat them in the way you eat your *dinner*,' I corrected him, 'but it DOES digest the essential *elements* that it needs to sustain life. The *husk* of the fly is discarded, in the same way that *we* discard the *solids* from our food. The *plant* however, doesn't need a *digestive system* like ours. In fact, it's simpler, and much more *efficient!* It takes in exactly what it requires ...'

'And it doesn't need to go to the toilet!' Frank added, much to Les's disgust!

'*Really* Frank!' He protested, 'Do you *have* to be so crude?'

'He's not being crude.' I sprang to Frank's defence. 'He's just stating a *fact!*'

I dropped a piece of meat into one of the traps, and it snapped shut.

'Yes, all right Pete,' Les conceded, 'but this is just a *curiosity*, isn't it? I mean, you don't see ROSES catching flies and eating them, *do you?*'

'In a sense, *all* plants eat living matter,' I replied, 'in the form of humus, the rotting remains of plants, animals, and even *humans!*'

'So when you're *dead*, Les,' Frank interrupted, 'you'll not only be *worm* fodder, but food for *plants, too!*'

Les seemed rather repulsed at the idea. He relit his pipe again, sending clouds of smoke spiralling to the roof of the greenhouse.

'I hope your plants don't mind the *smoke*.' He mocked. 'I wouldn't want to *upset* them!'

'Why not let the *plants* answer that question for *themselves?*' I suggested. 'Try blowing your smoke over this *mimosa* plant.'

Les, believing I was trying to send him up, rose to the challenge.

He blew a stream of smoke directly towards the mimosa. He was astonished when the plant's leaf axils dropped and the leaflets folded up neatly, out of the way of the invading smoke.

'I don't believe it!' He commented half to himself.

'Do you *STILL* think plants have no reasoning?' I asked as I switched the fan heater on. 'Now watch that *telegraph plant* in the corner ...'

As the heat wafted towards the plant, it's leaves started moving. They moved slowly at first, but then gradually started to speed up as the temperature increased. Eventually, the leaves were moving around in all directions.

'I've never seen anything like *that* before!' He gasped in wonder. 'Why does it do *that*?'

'Because it's *hot* of course!' I told him. 'Don't *YOU* fan yourself when you're hot?'

Les sat down and looked at all the plants around him for a few minutes.

'You know Pete,' He admitted, 'you've just opened up a whole new world to me. I've been so tied up with business matters lately, I seem to have lost touch with the very essence of life itself.

'I'll tell you what. I've got a few hours to spare. How about letting me in on some of the secrets of the plant world? Open my *mind* up a bit. Push all these *business worries* aside for a while?'

Frank glanced at me and grinned.

'Ok mate.' I agreed, 'let's go indoors and have a cuppa ...'

My wife Shirley made some tea for all four of us, and we settled down in the armchairs. 'Now then,' I said to Les, 'where would you like me to *start*?'

'At the *beginning* I suppose.' He suggested.

That, dear reader, is exactly where is I started ...

... AND HERE FOR YOUR BENEFIT, IS THE STORY WHICH CHANGED LES'S WHOLE OUTLOOK ON LIFE.

PART ONE

THE STORY OF PLANT LIFE

(AND ALL THAT FOLLOWED)

Cosmic Dust

Chapter One:

The Dawn Of Life

Everything in the Universe is living matter, and everything, from solar systems to the tiniest molecule, begin their physical life from a seed made up of a single cell.

Everything is made up of the same 92 elements, though everything in the universe originally began with only 2 elements, hydrogen and helium, the oldest elements in the universe. The *other* elements came about through the gentle force of gravitation, which pulled these atoms together, causing great compression and heat, which transformed these two elements, combining them into various permutations, until the complete 92 elements were created.

The first three elements created from hydrogen and helium were carbon, nitrogen and oxygen, and everything has developed from these. For example, water, a liquid, is made up of Hydrogen and Oxygen (H_2O).

Because of this, the Ancient Art of Alchemy (turning, for example, lead into gold, is, in principle, absolutely possible, though we couldn't possibly produce enough energy to make it work!

The biggest mystery of the universe is not what we *can* see, but what we *can't!*

This is what is called 'dark matter'. This makes up 85% of the entire universe! This follows that the 'light' matter or atomic matter, (our own existence) only accounts for 15% of the universe! This had not been realised until recently, because like attracts like: We, being made of 'light' or atomic matter, will automatically look for light (atomic) matter. Looking through a telescope, we would naturally look at the *bright* objects, - stars and the like: Why would we look at *dark* matter? To us, there is nothing there, - and yet this dark matter is what is actually there, - dark matter is a force in itself!

This dark matter is made up of enigmatic material which cannot be seen, smelled, tasted or touched, but which can travel through atomic (light) matter (even complete planets), without having any effect on either the dark or light matter.

What we *do* know is that this dark matter is what actually powers the universe, and regulates it.

This dark matter fills what we think of as empty space (which isn't empty at all!) It contains Dark Energy, which is anti-gravitational matter that works with gravitational matter to keep things in balance.

Whilst the light (atomic) matter attracts everything to it due to its gravitational pull, the dark matter, on the other hand, repels it: This causes a 'pulsating' effect, keeping everything alive: This is the heartbeat of the Universe!

Dark energy is the Key to understanding The Universe. It may be that this dark energy, which appears to control and create life causing the heartbeat of the universe is The Creator, God, or The Boss – a daunting thought!

Interestingly, the Ancients knew that the dark side of things is equally important as the light side, hence the symbol of Ying & Yang!

When a star begins to die, it firstly expands into a red giant, before collapsing within itself to become a white dwarf. It then continues to collapse until it becomes so dense that it becomes a black hole, which takes everything into it. (It, Too, is anti-gravitational, as happens with dark matter).

Before collapsing entirely however, it emits a ring of gases, which contain 'seeds' the essential material for the birth of new stars.

Over billions of years, these 'seeds' form new stars, some with planets orbiting around them, just as our star, the Sun, has planets orbiting around it.

Each planet then has the material to form other life, whether it is animal or plant life as we know it, or some other form of life that we do not yet understand.

Each of those life forms then produces seeds, or egg-cells, or spores, in order to reproduce, just as the star that gave it life in the first place did.

This cycle will be repeated over and over again, making our own existence appear pretty meaningless, but it isn't!

Everything on Earth (including us!) is actually made up of the nuclear waste from the stars, which is a bit of a sobering thought! Furthermore, if we are made up of the light (atomic) matter, it would follow that we really do have an inner light (as the Ancients believed again!) So when we die, does this inner light (The Spirit) return to the stars from whence it came, as, indeed, our bodies return to the Earth from whence *it* came? Ashes to ashes, dust to dust!

Scientists estimate that the planet Earth started forming some five thousand million years ago from a ball of burning gases thrown out into space in a great celestial explosion.

Gradually this burning mass cooled, through boiling liquid form, to a red-hot lump of rock, millions of years later.

Vapours were released from the hardening rock surface of the newly-formed planet, to form a dense atmosphere of gases. Most of these gases would have been *poisonous* to most of *today's* forms of life.

These vapours started to condense as the Earth cooled further. This condensation caused torrential rain, which continued for many thousands of years. These super monsoons eventually formed the seas and the oceans of the planet.

The great continents (though vastly different from today) were left to emerge above the water-line. These huge chunks of land were attached to huge plates of rock under the waters. These plates, the *Teutonic plates*, were formed by the cracking of the earth's surface as the crust cooled.

The plates in turn, floated upon the still red-hot liquid of the Earth's interior. The movements of these plates account for the changes in the shapes and locations of the continents through what is now known as '*continental drift*'.

The movements of these plates *also* account for the formation of the Earth's mountain rages, as the plates slid *under*, or crashed *into* each other with enormous force. This pushed up the Earth's crust as they did so, forming the mountain ranges.

Probably about three thousand million years ago, the Earth continued to cool, and many chemical changes took place, within the waters, and in the atmosphere of the young planet.

Carbon was formed from permutations of gases such as oxygen, carbon dioxide and carbon monoxide. Further computations of carbon and other chemicals eventually produced traces of nucleic acid, the basis of *all life.*

It really didn't take long in terms of evolution, for the nucleic acids to arrange themselves into strings of genes, the *designing factors* of life.

Frank suggests these were the first *'designer genes!'*

These strings of genes, in an effort to protect themselves from the hostile environment around them, formed *cases* around themselves. In this way, they eventually became the first *living cells* on this planet. They eventually went on to inhabit both water and atmosphere.

The very first seeds of life had been planted! Amoebas and plankton inhabited the seas, whilst bacteria and viruses inhabited the moist atmosphere.

It may by difficult for us to understand how these microscopic creatures were able to *exist* on such a newly-formed and hostile planet. Right across the young earth's surface were boiling springs. The atmosphere was sulphur-laden, due to earthquakes and volcanic activity.

To us mere humans, such an environment would be our worst nightmares. There is no way any form of animal life could exist in such conditions. As far as these first inhabitants of earth are concerned however, this is perfectly feasible. Even today, there are bacteria such as *Thiospirellum* species, and certain *algae,* which actually live and *thrive* in such conditions.

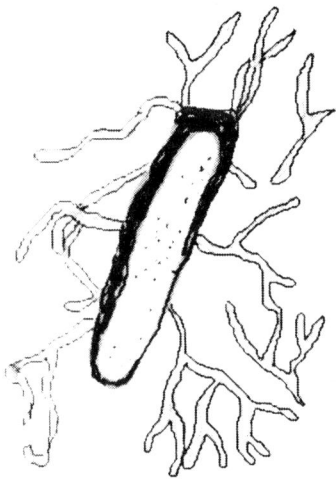

Bacteria

Indeed, to *some* forms of microscopic life, *OXYGEN* is lethal! We should remember too that, at this time, most of the very small amounts of oxygen on Earth were locked up in the *seas*.

These tiny but tough microscopic creatures were neither true *plants* nor true *animals* in the sense that we usually understand them, and yet they were the beginnings of *both*!

Many of these unicellular beings were capable of *photosynthesis* (the process by which plants convert Sunlight into energy), and yet they were *independently mobile*! In *today's* terms, they could be described either as *mobile plants*, or *photosynthetic animals*!

Plants and animals became a little more clearly defined, however, as those single cells started to form themselves into *colonies*. The amoeba and plankton cells became *sponges, jellyfish* and *algae*, whilst the *bacteria* and *viruses* formed *moulds*, growing upon the cooling masses of rocks upon the surface of the Earth.

It is interesting to note that

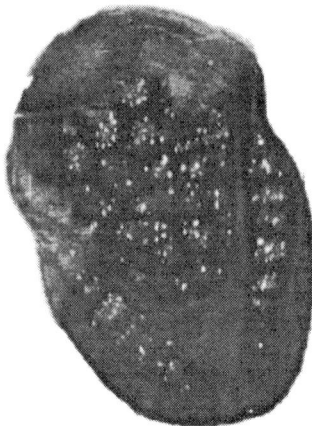

Mallomonus Zellensis
(Plankton)

20

fossils of algae have been found on rocks which are known to be over *two thousand million years old!*

As the moulds died, so others replaced them. Over many thousands of years they had formed a thin layer of *humus* all over the Earth's surface.

The creatures of the waters *also* formed similar layers on the *sea bed*, and on the bottom of the newly-formed rivers and lakes.

During this time, the Sun's rays were beginning to break through the thick layers of sulphur-laden clouds, to cast it's light upon the surface of the planet. This would have proved *lethal* to many of the microscopic creatures of the Earth. Many died out whilst others survived. This was due to the chemical computations which had evolved within their genetic make-up.

This phenomena is known nowadays as '*selective evolution*' or '*survival of the fittest*'.

Blue/green algae were the most *successful* of these mutations, as they were capable of living on the minute particles of *oxygen* in the waters, as well as the *carbon dioxide,* which was by this time, abundant.

They were also capable of using *Sunlight* to make *energy* (*photosynthesis*).

Very soon, some of the *algae* molecules were taken into the cells of *other* organisms, both from the water and the land. These went on to become the first true plants, containing *chloroplasts* (the green pigmentation of plants). This occurred through the algal molecules lodging themselves into the cells.

Moulds, made up of photosynthetic bacteria, soon adapted themselves to form *mosses, liverworts* and *lichen,* whilst others formed *fungi.* Together, these plants probably covered the Earth's surface in much the same way that grasses do today.

These lived upon the rich deposits of humus, which had been formed by the dead and decaying moulds which had preceded them.

With the coming of the new green plants, there occurred also a new form of reproduction. This was by means of the scattering of *spores,* rather than by simple cell division.

Somewhere along the way there must have been a union between some of the *algal* plants and the *fungal* plants. Even *today*, we find, in certain lichens, both fungal *and* algal cells.

Meanwhile in the seas, *other* algae were teaming up with colonies of cells to produce *seaweeds* and *pondweeds*.

Everything on Earth was soft and lush by this time, even though the Earth trembled with violent activity from earthquakes, volcanoes and hot water geysers.

The mosses and the fungi of the land, so far uninterrupted by any form of animal life, *thrived*. The plant's sole companions on the Earth's surface were the colonies of bacteria and viruses. These helped break down the remains of dead plants, to form humus, rich in essential nutrients, upon which the new race of plants could feed.

This was an early example of *symbiosis*, in which one life form is totally dependent upon another life-form, for the benefit of each others' very existence.

This was to become the basis of natural law. A law that all forms of life would follow instinctively. To *ignore* that law, would be to threaten the very essence of life upon the planet!

A *different* problem was now fast emerging. What with all the new green plants absorbing carbon dioxide from the atmosphere and replacing it with oxygen, the atmosphere of Earth was rapidly becoming laden with oxygen! This was a deadly gas to many tiny life forms and, of course, to the *plants themselves*!

The plants needed *carbon dioxide*, and plenty of it!

If the *oxygen* content outweighed the *carbon dioxide* content, the new race of green plants would suffocate, by breathing *lethal doses of oxygen*!

What was needed was something to *equalize the balance* by inhaling the oxygen which the plants exhaled, and replacing it with carbon dioxide, so that the plants could thrive.

Necessity is the mother of invention, and such a system was already beginning to evolve.

In the seas, small marine life began to emerge, which were capable of breathing oxygen and exhaling carbon dioxide. Oxygen was *plentiful* in the seas and rivers, as water is made up of *oxygen and hydrogen* molecules (H_2O).

The carbon dioxide released by the marine life was released from the water, into the atmosphere, whilst some of it was retained by the marine plants, in order to live. Naturally, these new marine creatures had to feed on *something,* and that was the *plankton,* their *own forefathers*!

Until this time, plants had been extremely simple in their structure. The plankton and bacteria were *one-celled units.* The moulds, mosses, algae and fungi were *colonies* of cells, living together to form independent units.

The *land plants* took nutrients from the soil by mean of long white threads know as *mycelium.* This penetrated the humus, taking the nutrients from it.

The *water plants* merely floated in, or on top of the water, taking vital elements from their liquid environment. There were, however, no plants at *that* time, which had actual *roots* as we know them today. That was until the first *ferns* appeared, about five hundred million years ago.

Although, like their predecessors, they reproduced by mean of *spores,* they *DID* have simple roots, green leaves, and semi-wooden stems.

They also brought *sex* to the Earth, with male and female organs. The *female* parts were fertilised by the *male* parts, and they released their spores through *cones.*

This transformation took place through the *mosses,* which had developed lush fern-like growth, the likes of which can be seen today in the moss, *Thudium tamariscinum.*

The actual ferns *themselves* were probably similar to *Selaginella,* which still exists today in the humid, tropical regions of the Earth.

Plants were now completely colonising the waters and land of Earth. They formed luxuriant growth, multiplying by means of simple division, or by the casting of spores. There were, as yet, no trees, shrubs or flowers. These early plants had the Earth to themselves. There was nothing to threaten their existence, apart from the awesome power within the bowels of the Earth itself. Boiling springs, volcanoes and earthquakes formed the only outside threat to their success. Ironically, the only *other* threat came from the activities of the plants *themselves* in using up the essential carbon dioxide, and replacing it with the gas which was lethal to them, *oxygen*!

Earth was an extremely hostile world. Yet it had given birth to lush pastures of moss, lichen, fungi and ferns. A thick layer of humus-rich soil was being built up all over land and in the waters, just waiting for it's potential to be fully realised.

The *horsetails* probably made their first appearance at about this time, (five hundred million years ago), taking the fern one stage further. These represented miniature *conifers* in some species, and primitive *grasses* in others.

There also emerged a group of plants known as the *psilophytes*, which were anchored to the soil by underground *rhizomes*, or storage

Horsetails

organs. These, too, were like primitive grasses or dwarf conifers, growing as they did, to a maximum of two feet.

This group of plants are now extinct, but specimens exist in museums, as carefully preserved fossils.

In the *seas*, the marine life was now growing larger, Fish and reptiles began to appear, and they fed upon the aquatic plant life.

Of course, there were better pickings in the lush pastures of the *land* now. The atmosphere upon the planet's surface was rapidly becoming rich in oxygen.

Now it was only a matter of time before the reptiles in the seas adapted themselves to life upon the *land*, to feed upon the lush plant growth which thrived there, and to breathe the abundance of sweet, unadulterated oxygen in the atmosphere.

At *this* stage, the plants were still only tapping into a very small depth of the thick layer of humus which had built up over thousands of years. Now, however, those plants were being threatened by the new invasion of *land animals* emerging from the seas.

The emergence of land animals was certainly *essential* to the plant life, in order to maintain the balance of gases. The problem was, that the animals would have to *feed* on something!

Their staple diet was the *plants themselves!*

This meant that the plants would have to dig in deeper, and grow stronger, if they were to survive the voracious appetites of the land animals!

The stage was set then, for the big battle for survival between the plants and the animals.

THE AGE OF THE GIANTS WAS ABOUT TO DAWN ...

Chapter Two:

THE AGE OF THE GIANTS!

One hundred million years ago, a giant dragonfly glides through the humid atsmosphere of the Earth. It flies past tree-like ferns, and horsetails of gigantic proportions. The repties are just developing into creatures of massive proportions. this heralds the age of the giants ...

Until this time, there had been ferns, horsetails and the psilophytes, growing amongst the mosses and lichens which covered the Earth's surface. Now, however, there were changes taking place among the *ferns*.

Some species were now producing *seeds* rather than *spores*.

These were the now-extinct *seed-ferns*, known only to modern science as fossil remains, and known to scientists as *Neuropteris* and *Lyginopteris*.

All of these plants grew to a maximum of two feet. There was, however, now a thick layer of good rich humus to be used. The threat, for the first time since life developed, to land plants by marauding animals, meant that the plants had to penetrate their roots further into the soil. They also had to send their vital leaves up higher towards the sky, so that they were out of the reach of the animals.

Tree ferns

Ferns adapted their leaf-axils and roots to form crude trunks. This gave rise to the *tree ferns*. Some species of these still exist today, and can reach heights of up to 30 feet in the *dioon* species, to 60 feet in the *cyathea* species.

The *horsetails* too, found it desirable to go in an upwardly mobile direction! Some, like the now extinct *Crucalamites*, grew to a height of some *NINETY FEET*!

The *Cycads* were a group of plants springing from the *seed-ferns*, which became giants, along with the dinosaurs. Although they did not produce *trunks*, the *leaves themselves*, reached a height of *eight feet* or more!

Cycads

These were the first tree-like plants on Earth, although they still reproduced by means of spores released from cones, rather than by seed. Some of these cones were giants in *themselves*, especially those of the Cycads, whose upright cones were as long as the eight-foot leaves!

As the *plants* continued to grow in size, so did the *creatures of the land and sea*. It was like a race between animals and plants, to see which could outgrow the other!

There was the *brontosaurus*, larger than a double-decker bus, and easily capable of reaching the succulent leaves of the tree-ferns and the horsetails, as well as grazing upon the lush pastures of grasses and mosses.

To *combat* this onslaught by the giant reptiles, the *psilophytes* produced trees with needle-like leaves. This was the beginning of the true conifers, *Pines, Junipers, Yews*, and the forerunner of the Monkey-puzzle tree, *Araucaria araucana*. This is probably one of the most successful *anti-marauder* trees ever to have evolved!

Some of these conifers, in the desperate attempt to outgrow the dinosaurs, went on to reach an incredible 300 feet!

Out of all this, a conifer emerged, maybe by pure chance, or maybe by natural selection, which bore *BROAD* leaves, almost heart-shaped in fact , of a leathery texture. This was a great departure from the needlelike leaves of previous trees.

Due to the larger surface area of the leaves however, it was more efficient at catching the rays of the sun, for the purpose of photosynthesis.

This tree was the Maidenhair tree, *Ginkgo*, which, although still a conifer (cone-bearer), it produced crude male and female *'flowers'*, and used *pollen* as a fertilizer.

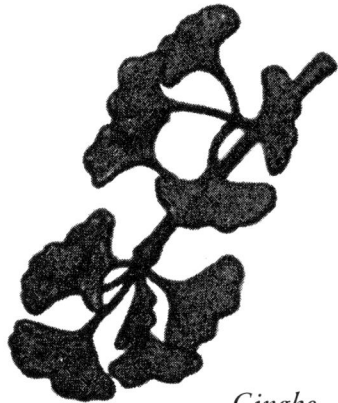

Gingko

The cones were rather more like little round *nuts* than actual *cones*, but these contained true *seeds*.

The only example of this tree still in existence today is *Ginkgo biloba*. Indeed, this species would certainly have become extinct, if it had not caught the attention of an ancient Chinese Emperor, who cultivated it in his garden thousands of years ago.

Perhaps that emperor was the first conservationist!

Developing from the Ginkgo, a whole race of broad-leaved trees and plants made an appearance upon the Earth's surface. Some of these produced succulent fruits.

With this development, the plants had hit upon a way of using the animals for their own benefit!

These fruits would be eaten by the animals, although the *seeds*, too tough for digestion, would be released via the *droppings* of the animals.

By the time the indigestible seed had been discarded in this way, the animal may have travelled several miles from the parent plant.

This ensured a wider distribution of the trees, and marked the beginning of symbiosis (where two or more different organisms work together for mutual benefit), between the true *plants* and the true *animals*. It was as though the plant life had at last accepted the coming of the animals and taken the view '*if you can't beat' em, join 'em !*'

Until this time, all the reptiles which walked the earth were *herbivores* (plant eaters).

The production of fruit not only satisfied the appetites of the *animals*, but also ensured *seed distribution*, leaving the vital *leaves* of these plants to do the jobs of respiration, transpiration and photosynthesis.

Some plants, unable to cope with the feeding frenzy of these animals, became extinct. Others had to adapt themselves in order to withstand the insatiable appetites of the giant creatures.

The balance was shifting, and the dinosaurs were in danger of becoming so widespread as to destroy all the plant life on Earth!

Nature had, once more, to equalize the balance.

If all the *plant life* was destroyed, the *animals* would rapidly follow the same fate.

The problem was not only the fact that they would no longer have anything to *eat*, but there would be no more plants left, to convert the carbon dioxide into oxygen! The animals which didn't die of *starvation*, would soon die of *suffocation*!

To counteract this imbalance, nature, in her wisdom, developed a race of blood-thirsty *carnivores* (meat-eaters). These were giant dinosaurs which attacked and ate the plant eaters.

The fiercest of these, as any schoolchild will know, was the aptly-named *Tyrannosaurus Rex* (The King of the Tyrants).

Ironically, although the carnivores kept a check on the *plant-eaters*, their activities posed yet *another* threat to the plant life they were created to help protect!

As these giant reptiles fought for life and limb, they would crush plants and knock down trees!

Other developments would have to take place if the plants were to continue their fight for survival!

The *Tree-ferns* developed into long slender *palm trees,* which would bend under the weight of the animals, and then whip back up into position.

The *conifers* became even *larger*, *stronger* and *firmer* at the roots. The *Sequoia* (giant redwoods) developed, growing to a height of 350 to 400 feet. Their massive trunks could easily withstand the weight of the dinosaurs' huge bodies. To help cushion the blows even further, their trunks were of a *spongy* nature, so that not even a crack in the bark would occur!

Some of the reptiles took to the air as in the case of the *pterodactyls*, whilst others became *smaller*, enabling them to hide from the flesh-eaters in the undergrowth.

Many of them developed markings on their skins to act as camouflage, whilst others became warm-bloooded mammals, giving birth to, and suckling, live young, rather than hatching them from eggs.

This development at least prevented the predators from stealing eggs, for the developing youngsters were always carried with their mothers inside their wombs!

Of course, the Earth was still continuing to cool, and the live-born youngsters would need some protection on their bodies to keep then warm. Hence the first furry animals made their debut.

Being warm-blooded also had the added advantage of *speed* during cold spells.

Cold-blooded creatures such as the dinosaurs became *sluggish* in cold periods. The *warm-blooded* animals, on the other hand, were able to maintain their body temperatures, *whatever* the outside temperatures. This meant that they were faster, and more agile. They could *escape* from the cold-blooded hunters.

Plants developed new methods of adapting to the changing face of the Earth too. Some took to living in the swamps and bogs which were now widespread across the Earth. Dinosaurs and other animals ventured into these areas at their peril! Here, the rotting vegetation that had built up over millions of years was constantly soaked. It formed an inert form of humus called *peat*.

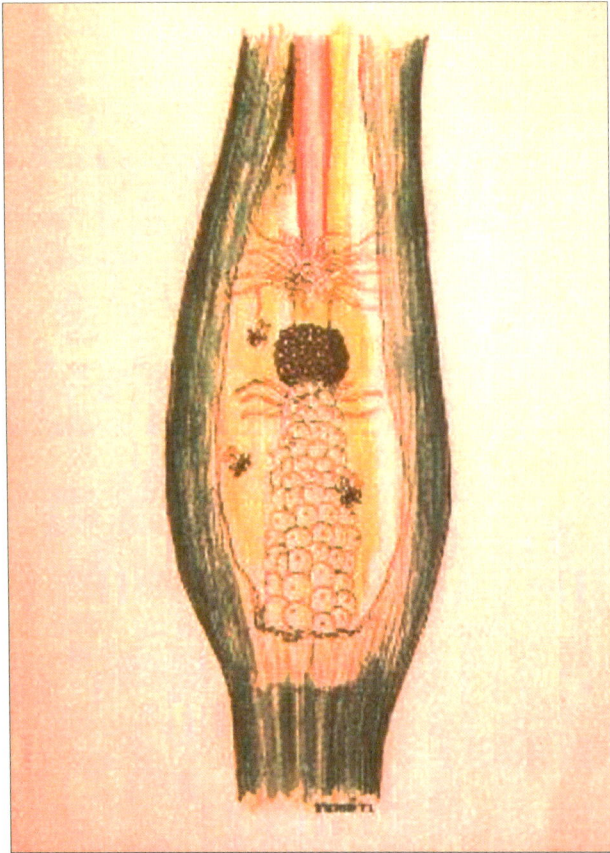

Flies trapped in spathe of Arum

Here in the peat bogs, there were not enough nutrients available to sustain plant life, so a race of plants developed, which would turn the tables somewhat on the plant-eating animals!

The leaves of these plants developed into *traps* of varying types. These traps were capable of ensnaring insects, small lizards and amphibians. In fact, any animal that was light enough to walk on the soft peat bogs, or was capable of flying. 'Baits' were developed by the plants, which would help to lure their prey. The plants produced a sweet sticky liquid, which their prey would find irresistible.

Once the prey was trapped, either by means of a snapping trap, a sticky surface or a 'pitcher' of liquid with smooth sides to prevent escape, the plants would digest all the nutrients it needed from the insect or animal at it's leisure. The fleshy 'husk' of the unfortunate prey was discarded.

Today, there still exists several species of these carnivorous plants. These include the Venus' fly trap, the sundews, the pitcher plants and the bladderworts.

As the plants became more sophisticated, so they made increasing use of the insects. Not quite in the same way as the 'carnivorous' plants though.

In the case of the *non*-carnivorous plants, the insects were made use of for *fertilization* purposes. Indeed, even the flowering species of *carnivorous* plants made use of them in this way.

The broad-leaved ferns gave rise to the *Arums*.

Insects, (mainly flies) are attracted by the carrion-like smell emitted from many of these plants. They then become trapped inside the hooded *spathe* (a flower-like structure).

As the insect flies about trying to escape, they dislodge the pollen from the spadix (male reproduction organ), which would then fall on to the stigma (female reproductive organ) and so, fertilise the seeds.

From here on, a whole range of flowering plants began to develop.

Some of the *plantains*, *horsetails* and *psilohytes* gave rise to the true flowering *grasses*, which were so hardy and abundant that they could not only withstand the constant fights between the Giant reptiles and new mammals, but even the constant grazing of the herbivores.

Some seventy million years ago, the dinosaurs, not being able to withstand the cooling temperatures of the Earth, finally became extinct after dominating the planet for over two hundred million years!

An ice age gripped the Earth. Only the most adaptable plants and animals were able to survive. Hibernation, plus a covering of thick fur and warm blood, helped the animals through this period.

Plants which had an inbred hardiness, and the ability for their seeds to remain 'viable' for some 500,000 years (the total length of the Ice Age !) also survived.

It was a time for the earth to sort out the most *beneficial* life-forms for it's own survival, from the most *destructive*.

The dinosaurs had outgrown their usefulness. *They had to go!*

As the Ice finally receded, the Earth became warm again. The planet became once more, amass with plants and trees of many varied species.

There were also many mammals and small reptiles. The flying reptiles, adapting to the changing temperatures, had now developed feathers as a protection from the cold.

The first *birds* took to the air.

THE EARTH WAS NOW IN THE RIGHT CONDITION FOR THE INTRODUCTION OF A <u>CARETAKER</u> …

Chapter Three:

MAN - THE EARTH'S CARETAKER!

The great ice age had at last wiped the giant dinosaurs off the face of the earth. As the ice subsided, the planet became a warm, lush place in which to live once more …

During this great freeze, such animals as the woolly Rhinoceros, the Mammoths and Mastodons had evolved.

They had been perfectly adapted to the freezing conditions during the ice age, with their long shaggy fur coats. They were able to exist upon the plants which were hardy enough to survive the Arctic conditions.

These animals were, in fact, the largest animals to survive through the ice age. As conditions began to improve again, they gradually dispensed of their woolly coats, evolving into the rhinos and elephants that we know today.

Some of the smaller *meat-eating* animals survived too, and these gave rise to the *felines* such as the *smilodon*, or *sabre-tooth as some call it*.

This short, stumpy early ancestor of lions and tigers had large sabre-like teeth, which were probably used for stabbing their prey. Unfortunately, it seems likely that these tusk-like teeth continued to grow, so that eventually, as the cat became older, the teeth would have been more of a *hindrance* than an *asset!*

There were also *canines* such as the *wolf* and the *wild dog*.

The plants, ever ready to meet a challenge, made full use of these new furry creatures, by producing seeds with 'barbs', which would stick to the fur of these animals, to be transported many miles away. Eventually, the animal would lay down in the grass, fight, or scratch itself. The seeds would fall onto the ground where they would germinate.

One group of animals, the *primates,* or *apes and monkeys*, found the perfect refuge from predators. They took to living in the trees. In this environment, they became perfect athletes. This was due to the development of *prehensile* (clinging) *hands, feet* and, in the case of the monkeys, *tails*.

They also developed *opposing thumbs*, which allowed them to grip objects of various shapes and sizes.

One form of ape took to living on *ground* however. They sought refuge from their enemies by living in natural caves, which had been formed in the rocks by the expansion of ice during the Ice Age.

Because of the comparative weakness and lack of speed of this species, they had to rely largely upon their wits in order to survive.

As a result, they developed a keen brain. Thanks to their opposing thumbs, they learned how to make and to use *tools* and *weapons*.

Due to this constant use of the hands, they took to walking upright. This left their hands free for food foraging, and in order to defend themselves. This ape was the first animal to do so constantly.

Homo Erectus, the Upright Man had arrived.

As Man's ability to make implements grew, so did his self-confidence. This meant that he could hunt and kill animals much *larger* than himself, providing him with food and clothing.

He discovered how to produce and use *fire*. With this, he could keep warm in cold weather, cook meat, and keep dangerous animals away from the entrance of the cave.

He began to use *intellect*, using the pigmentation from plants to make *cave paintings*.

Many of these depicted *hunting scenes*. He had learned that plants could be used for purposes other than merely for food. He learned that the *teeth and bones* of animals could be used, not only for tools and weapons, but also for decorative purposes.

The first *necklaces* were probably worn in order to impress his fellows regarding his hunting prowess.

He began to reason, and to wonder about his own existence, becoming the first animal ever to do so.

This was *Homo Sapiens*, or *Intelligent Man*. He first walked the Earth some *three million years ago*.

The dinosaurs may have been the *longest-surviving* creatures on Earth. Man though, was certainly the *fastest-developing*!

Very soon, he was capable of discovering a *variety* of things to eat, both animal *and* vegetable.

He learned how to put many of the Earth's *resources* to his own use. *Stones and bones* were used for making *tools, weapons and jewellery*. Animal skins were used for *clothing*. Flower pigments were used, not only for *painting*, but also for decorating their *bodies and clothing*. Mankind even developed an ability to train *other* animals to help with his hunting and for his own protection.

Naturally, this relationship evolved over thousands of years.

Basically, Man would follow packs of *wild dogs*.

In the *first* instances, he would probably attempt to *steal* from the dogs, for Man was an *opportunist*, a scavenger who, like the *vultures and hyenas*, would leave it to the stronger animals to do the killing.

As Man learned to make, and use *weapons*, such as *spears*, however, he would *help* the dogs to kill their quarry from a distance.

This slowly developed into a partnership, Man and the dogs sharing the meal between them.

This was yet *another* example of Symbiosis, and part of nature's plan for a balanced existence.

Mankind, having gained the *trust* of the dogs, allowed them to share their caves. This began a long relationship with dogs which still exists to this day.

Man was now well on his way to realising his potential as 'The Earth's Caretaker'. An intelligent being who, because of his superior intelligence and power of reason, could nurture the planet and keep everything '*in balance*'

This seemed to be Man's destiny, and in the early days, everything went according to plan …

Somewhere along the way it appears, Mankind developed into two separate species.

It was originally thought that from the very rugged *Neanderthal man*, developed the more artistic *cro-magnon* man.

Recent DNA research however, suggests that modern man is not even *related* to Neanderthal man! So where does that leave us?

We know that the two species lived side-by-side upon the earth for some time, and that Neanderthal man suddenly became extinct.

It is possible that cro-magnon man, *homo sapiens*, or *thinking* man, had something to do with his extinction.

Since *Neanderthal man* became extinct soon after the appearance of *cro-magnon* man, plus the fact that he did not evolve from that species, it leaves us with the intriguing problem of where *homo sapiens* came from!

Whatever. From here on, Homo sapiens made incredible advances.

Some ten thousand years ago, a group of *homo sapiens* took to a nomadic lifestyle, following the migration patterns of herds of grazing animals such as buffalo.

This way, they had a constant supply of fresh meat and milk. Eventually the men gained the trust of these beasts, and they took to leading them to pastures of their own choosing.

About eight thousand years ago, Men in the Middle East took to growing grasses in special fields. These were the first primitive farmers. As mankind migrated North, he had to rely more and more on these cereal crops, as the lush fruits of the tropics were no longer available to him.

Interestingly, it is thought that the white skins of the *northern* races is due to this large intake of cereal crops.

Fruit gives us essential vitamin C, which is not found in sufficient quantities in cereal crops.

Without this essential vitamin, Man is prone to *rickets*. Vitamin C *is* present however, in *Sunlight*. Nature, in her infinite wisdom, took away the sun-protecting black pigments of this new northern man's skin, in order to allow more *Sunlight* to filter through.

If this theory is *correct,* then white Man has been in existence for less than ten thousand years, being a mutation of the original *dark-skinned* man.

The first evidence we have of Mankind actually *breeding* plants in order to yield better crops comes from Jericho, about five thousand years ago. Several hybrid grasses appeared, bearing grain which was too heavy to blow away on the wind.

This was almost certainly due to natural crossing and mutation, rather than conscious selective breeding on the part of the humans.

The Men of Jericho however, seeing the advantage of the larger grain, (which would not be lost in the wind, and were easier to harvest), began to grow only *these new types* of cereal.

By selective breeding, they produced a cereal crop that was the forerunner of modern corn, barley, wheat and rye.

From here on, Man discovered that by this method of selective breeding (a step on from natural selection), he could improve other useful crops.

On he went to produce selected strains of vegetables, fruits and *herbs*, which he found useful in medicinal potions, as well as in the improvement of food flavours.

It seems that the first attempts to raise plants purely for decorative purposes were in China, some four thousand years ago.

We have already seen, in chapter two, how a Chinese Emperor, with an eye for beauty, saved the Ginkgo tree from becoming extinct.

It is *also* this race of people who have given us the Hybrid Tea rose, and many varieties of Camellia, Azalea and Flowering Cherry.

It is almost certain that the Chinese, with their eye for beauty, have actually saved *other* plants from extinction.

The pot plant *primula obconica* has *NEVER* been found growing in the wild, and yet it has been prized as a garden plant in the Chinese province of Schezwan for at least two thousand years! It is either now completely extinct in the wild state, or it has been hybridized out of all recognition.

The *Japanese too*, are old masters of cultivation, especially in the art of *Bonsai* (dwarfing trees), which has been practised in that country since the thirteenth century. Surprisingly, this art, associated so much with Japanese culture, was originated in China centuries before! Even the word 'Bonsai' is of Chinese origin, meaning, literally, 'planted in a shallow vessel'.

The Chinese, regarding *nature itself* as the true God, would create microcosms of nature in these shallow bowls, and place them on household altars.

Because of Man's natural inquisitiveness and thirst for knowledge, he has continued to breed plants which bear little resemblance today, to their wild ancestors.

The modern floribunda and Hybrid Tea Rose bear little resemblance to any *wild* rose. The same applies to varieties of fuchsia, dahlia, chrysanthemum, and many others. We do know that, apart from Man's part in speeding up evolution, nature *itself* is still adapting plants and animals to suit a particular environment.

Indeed, the *environment* is constantly changing, as is the physical face of the planet *itself*.

Less than one million years ago, volcanic eruptions under the sea pushed up lava to above sea level. This formed a colony of islands, which, collectively, covered an area of 6,433 square miles!

Soon after these islands started cooling, plants began to colonise it. Seeds of nettle plants were blown, via freak winds, to these newly-formed islands. Finding conditions favourable, they adapted themselves to a life of luxury.

In less than one million years, these humble nettles have evolved into nettle *TREES* of gigantic proportions!

Over the millennia, the leaves have lost their stinging power. There was no point in wasting energy producing stinging leaves, for there were no *marauders* on the islands from which they had to *protect* themselves!

Plants were the only living creatures to exist on these islands until about 2,500 years ago, when *mankind* colonized it, bringing with him animals and birds. Those islands are known today as the *Hawaiian Islands*!

So plants were still adapting themselves for life in a changing environment. Mankind too, had been lending nature a hand in the improvement of species, not only of plants, but also of animals and birds, keeping in step with his predestined role as 'caretaker' of the planet.

Unfortunately, Man's quest for knowledge, and his own instincts for self-survival, led to *greed* and a total *disregard* for the planet and it's inhabitants. He cared only for those which suited his own selfish requirements.

In so doing, he began to upset the balance of the *planet itself.*

He was putting his OWN life in peril, together with all other life on the planet!

COULD MAN *REALLY* DESTROY ALL WHICH HAS TAKEN NATURE THOUSANDS OF MILLION OF YEARS TO CREATE, IN JUST A FEW HUNDRED YEARS, OR WILL HE SEE HIS MISTAKES IN TIME, AND TIP THE SCALES ONCE AGAIN TO BECOME THE TRUE 'CARETAKER OF THE PLANET' AS WAS HIS ORIGINAL HIS DESTINY?

PART TWO

TIPPING THE SCALES

Chapter Four

FROM CARETAKER TO PLUNDERER!

Man has become the undisputed Lord of Planet Earth. He has learned how to domesticate animals and cultivate plants, not only for practical uses, but also for his own pleasure. He has also plundered the natural resources from his only home in the universe, with disastrous effects!

Without the slightest forethought for the future, he has robbed the Earth of coal, peat and oil, for his own selfish purposes. He has been using up, within a few hundred years, that which the Earth has taken millions of years to form.

Likewise, he has plundered the Earth for it's rarest elements, precious stones, metals and minerals. Diamonds and rubies, gold and silver, so that the few who could *possess* these elements could gain power over his fellow humans.

Man has become infested with greed. Instead of becoming the planet's 'caretaker', he was fast becoming her greatest enemy.

As Man developed more sophisticated civilization, so a social structure, based upon the differences between those *with* power and those *without*, emerged. *Possessiveness* entered Man's nature, as he sought out symbols of power.

To *early* civilization, these were the teeth of the most ferocious animals. A great hunter who displayed these symbols gained respect, for if he could win a battle against such a *dangerous animal*, what mere member of his *own tribe* would dare challenge him? The first 'leaders of Men' emerged.

Other, more passive humans, discovered some of nature's secrets. The phases of the Sun and the Moon, the regularity of volcano eruptions, earthquakes, geysers and rainfall. They discovered the medicinal and hallucinatory effects of certain plants. They relied on *superstition* and *knowledge* for their respect within the tribes.

The witch doctors, medicine men and wise men emerged as advisors to the all-powerful leaders.

As Man continued to explore the Earth, he found that certain minerals were very scarce. Those lucky enough to find the rarest, - gems and precious metals, gained a form of power which was based upon wealth and greed. To have something that nobody *else* could have was deemed to be a power in itself.

Within any civilization, Men would agree to do *anything* for a piece of this new-found 'wealth'.

So arose the 'wealthy' and the 'poor', based on nothing more than an urge to claim nature's wealth for themselves.

Those who *had* wealth and power could dominate the poor into doing all the hard work for them. Of course, this included plundering the Earth even *further*, not only for gems and precious metals to act as 'status symbols' but also for *fossil fuels*. This included coal and peat for the *wealthy* to burn, so that they could gain more comfort from heat and cooking facilities.

The poor were rewarded for this work with small portions of this 'wealth' in the form of gold and silver. This could be used by the poor to obtain the *essentials* of life such as food and water. Because of the advent of civilization, these essentials were no longer the basic rights of all living things, as they had been before!

The once common land which *produced* these basic essentials had been claimed, and were now 'owned' by the wealthy.

The *produce* from this land, which nature had provided for *all*, now had to be 'earned' by the poor.

A basic 'currency' had arrived, and this marked the end of Mankind's basic respect for the planet, and all other life upon it.

'Wealthy' man owned tracts of land which nature had intended to be be shared by all. 'Poor' man however, was set to work to *farm* that land, and *build* upon it, in order to gain a little of the wealth provided by 'wealthy' man. This wealth, which 'poor' man had earned, then had to be returned to 'wealthy' man in order to pay for the crops and meat that 'poor' man had raised in the *first* place!

Mining and farming meant clearing acres upon acres of woodland and natural grassland. The resulting timbers from the woodland were sold for burning, paper making and the building of ships and houses.

Even the *trees* which had to be cleared to make way for profitable *farmland* made 'wealthy' Man even wealthier!

Trees became an even *greater* source of wealth as civilization grew.

By *this* time, bigger *ships* were being built, as too, were larger *houses*.

Even the *poor* had timber-built houses, and the *rich*, in order to keep ahead of the *poor*, demanded not only bigger *houses*, but finer, more ornate *furniture*.

Within *two hundred years*, more than *half* the great forests in the civilized world had been totally destroyed, together with much of it's wildlife.

The scales were beginning to tip the *wrong way* due to the greed of Mankind, and this was just the *beginning!*

With the *industrial revolution*, a period heralded in the history books as a giant step forward for Mankind was, in fact, a giant *setback* for the *planet!* Not only were more *forests and woodland* cleared away, but *upon* those sites were built factories and power stations, which burned even *more* fossil fuels.

To add insult to injury, they also used up more essential *oxygen* and replaced it with *carbon dioxide.* They *also* pumped into the atmosphere deadly gases such as *sulphur dioxide, nitrous oxide* and *carbon monoxide.*

Now the last three gases are deadly to *all* forms of life apart from a few viruses and bacteria, as we have already discussed in part one. Carbon dioxide, which is usually absorbed by green plants, was building up to dangerous levels in the atmosphere. This was because there weren't enough green plants left on Earth to convert this sudden influx of *carbon dioxide* into *oxygen,* the gas that is essential to *all* animal life, including *Mankind!*

Man, during his relatively short time on Earth, was rapidly turning back the clock towards the conditions that existed on Earth before the emergence of life.

Some Men of vision could *see* this, and yet Mankind as a race *STILL* continued on this reckless assault upon the Earth!

He started plundering the Earth *again* for *Iron Ore* and *other* base metals, in order to meet the demands of the Industrial Revolution. This was to enable him to build stronger and larger *ships* and *other* mechanical devices.

Steam trains were invented. These burned *more* fossil fuels and pumped out even more *carbon dioxide* into the atmosphere. Of course, more *trees and green plants* had to be destroyed in order to make way for *railway tracks* and *stations*.

The *motor car* and *other* internal combustion vehicles made their appearance, using up several times more oxygen than Man himself, or any other form of animal life. They pumped out not only carbon dioxide, but many other deadly gases, including more of one of the deadliest, *carbon monoxide*. This noxious gas kills *ALL* forms of life on this planet!

As if *that* weren't bad enough, he went on to introduce *aeroplanes*, and the *jet engine*, which does more damage to the environment than any *other* form of transport.

This is the point where Mankind's destruction of the planet *really* took a turn for the worse!

Motor vehicles needed *roads* on which to travel. This meant that more and more *forests, woodland* and *green plants* perished in it's wake. The motor car was now wealthy man's latest *status symbol*.

As poor man worked *harder* and demanded more share of the *wealth,* however, *he too*, wanted to own a motor car! This became possible when Henry Ford produced the first family car.

Wealthy man, ever anxious to maintain the *status quo*, reasserted his position by owning *bigger* cars, and *more of them*!

More trees and green plants were destroyed right across the civilized world. to make way for motorways, autobahns, freeways and municipal car parks.

In Mankind's frenzied fanaticism to own a car, private gardens were concreted or tarmaced over, to make way for this new 'metal guru'.

The car had become a total obsession, with all other considerations paling into insignificance.

This obsession, which has developed only within the last *ONE HUNDRED YEARS* is now pushing the scales to disastrous limits. We are building larger towns and cities, roads and motorways, and more and more motor *vehicles*.

In so doing, we are destroying more and more trees and *other* green plants, pumping out more and more deadly gases into our atmosphere, causing a hole in the Earth's protective ozone layer, and adding to the potentially disastrous 'Greenhouse effect'.

It is interesting that some of the terms used by modern man, when talking about the motor car, have a deadly ring of *truth* about them.

He says, of a particularly impressive car, 'it takes your breath away, doesn't it?' When saving up for his own personal 'dream machine' he will tell you, 'of course, it costs the *Earth* …'

Both are much closer to the truth than he realizes!

Sometimes, when Mankind decides to *study* the problems he is causing, he actually makes it *worse*!

When the hole in the ozone layer was discovered above Antarctica in the eighties, they actually sent up a *jet plane*, filled with sophisticated instruments, to *measure* the problem.

Didn't they even stop to consider that the emissions from the jet engine were actually *adding* to the problem?

Sometimes, I *despair* at Mankind's utter *stupidity*!

Even those who profess to enjoy *country life* have added to earth's problems!

Dogs, once Man's ally in self-preservation, have now been bred to glorify Mankind's domination of all other life around him.

There are dogs that are used as *status symbols*. The *lap dogs* of the rich, and the big fierce dogs of 'macho' man.

True, there are still *hunting dogs*, but instead of being used for mutual self-preservation, they are used for Mankind's destructive nature in *blood sports* together with that most noble of creatures, *the horse.*

Dogs and other animals are even used in cruel experiments to satisfy Mankind's craving for knowledge and supremacy.

Farmers and gardeners use Man-made *chemicals* to combat what he describes as *'pests* and *weeds'.*

In truth, these are merely the earth's creatures and plants, which are an essential part of the whole, but which do not happen to fit in with our ideals!

Gardeners even sweep up *leaves* (nature's own compost) from their gardens, *burn them,* and then buy *peat*, which has been plundered from the Earth, in order to replenish the humus content in the soil, which *he* had *destroyed* the *previous* season !

Can you think of anything more *futile*, and *wasteful?*

In the meantime, of course, millions of creatures *perish* as their natural homes, the *wetlands and peat bogs*, are *destroyed* !

Our only hope is to change our whole *outlook* in life, and look again at the world around us, to find out how it works for us ALL …

Carbon dioxide

Oxygen

1 oak tree equals 2 people

OXYGEN BALANCE
Oxygen - breathed by humans
Carbon dioxide - breathed by plants
Carbon monoxide - deadly to both

Oxygen

Carbon monoxide

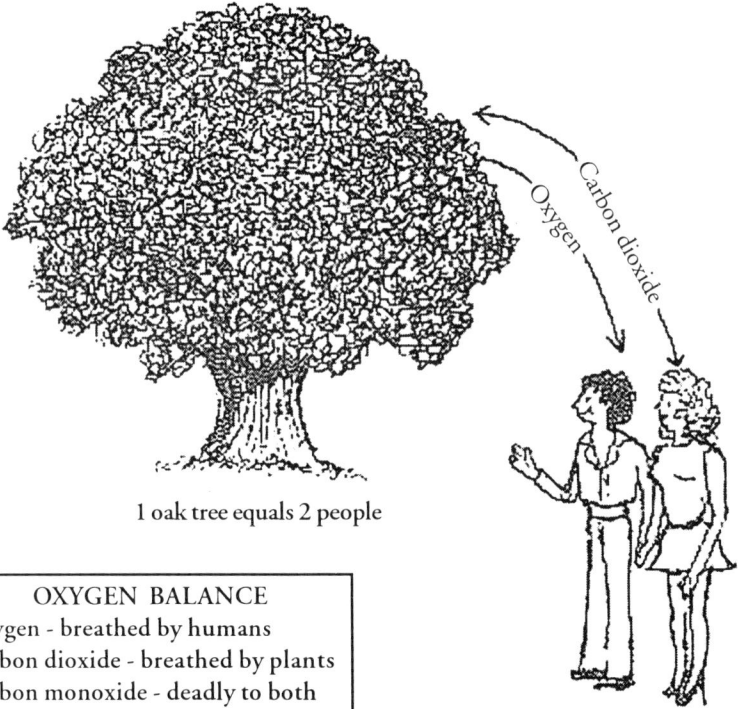

150 oak trees equals 1 small car

Chapter Five

TREE'S COMPANY!

A full-grown oak tree produces enough oxygen to keep two people alive. In other words if two people were put into a glass dome with one oak tree they would keep each other alive by the 'exchange of gases'. The tree *inhales* the carbon dioxide, which is *exhaled* by the humans. The tree then *exhales* oxygen, which is *inhaled* by the two people.

This is a very simplified example of the balance of gases. Generally speaking though, this constitutes a perfect balance. It represents a microcosm of the whole 'balance of nature'.

How then, does this compare with the motor car?

In order to keep a small car running continuously, it would take *NO FEWER THAN ONE HUNDRED AND FIFTY OAK TREES, TO SUPPLY THE CAR WITH ENOUGH OXYGEN!*

That means that *EVERY CAR ON THE ROAD TODAY USES 300 TIMES MORE OXYGEN THAN A HUMAN BEING!*

Unfortunately for all life on Earth, not only does the car convert some of this oxygen into *Carbon Dioxide*. It also emits several toxic gases, including *Carbon Monoxide*, which is deadly *to ALL FORMS LIFE ON THIS PLANET*. This means that those one hundred and fifty oak trees, if left in a confined space with the car, *WOULD BE DEAD WITHIN A COUPLE OF MONTHS!*

If we put our two people, together with the car, *and* one hundred and fifty-one oak trees together in that imaginary glass dome, not only would the trees be dead in a few months, so would the people!

Using this as a guide, you can imagine what motor vehicles *ALONE* are doing to our atmosphere!

On a *larger* scale, in order to keep a medium sized *power station* running, it would take a plantation of trees *THE SIZE OF GREATER LONDON!*

You see, if it were only *people and animals* that were using the oxygen content of this planet, there would probably be plenty of trees and green plants to keep us all alive, especially if we replaced the motorways with fields and woodlands.

Because Mankind chooses to live in this mechanical age of high-speed transport, central heating and mass-production however, we must do all in our power to ensure that our successors are able to breathe good, clean, oxygen-filled air.

Taking *lead* out of petrol *is* a step in the right direction. This is because lead has been proved to cause *brain damage*, either by being breathed in by Mankind and the animals (which is why vandalism is more common in built-up areas), or being absorbed by fruit and vegetables, to be *EATEN* by Mankind and the animals.

It is interesting to note that not only is *HUMAN* vandalism more rife in built-up areas. Town *BIRDS* are more likely to attack *garden flowers* such as primroses and crocuses, than their country cousins. It is thought that these 'townie' birds are suffering from *brain damage* as a direct result of *lead poisoning*! Unfortunately, lead in petrol is the *least* of our worries!

The *REAL* 'villain of the piece' is the deadly gas, *Carbon Monoxide*, which is present as much in *lead-free* petrol as any *other* !

When someone commits suicide by locking themselves into a sealed garage with a car engine running, the cause of death is NEVER by lead poisoning. It is always identified by coroners as 'death *Carbon Monoxide* poisoning.'

Are we to assume then, that it is OK to die of *Carbon Monoxide* poisoning, as long as we don't get brain damage from *LEAD poisoning*?

Catalytic converters fare rather better, although they *DO* use the Earth's precious metals, gold and silver, and they *STILL* use as much precious Oxygen. They are also *completely useless* on small, around-the-town journeys!

The hard truth is, if we continue to use the petrol-driven internal combustion engine, (even though there *are* several options), we MUST take a fresh look at the plants which supply us with all that essential oxygen. *Banning* petrol-driven engines would be by far the best option.

At one time, much of the British Isles was densely populated with trees. Hertfordshire in particular, was noted for its forests and woodlands.

The Chilterns were thickly covered by Beech trees, and so became the favourite haunts of robbers, who could hide in the shrubland, pouncing on their unsuspecting prey! A visitor to the Chilterns wrote in 1622, 'Here, if you beat a bush, it's odds on you'll start a thief!'

OK, so there *were* problems for the lone traveller, but can you imagine the sheer health-giving beauty of acres upon acres of *beech woods?*

The Beeches of the Chilterns gradually gave way to thickets and woods of silver birch, the tall and stately 'ladies of the wood'. In fact, the name of the Hertfordshire town of *Berkhamstead* actually translates to 'the homestead among the birches'. The town was originally one of the chief residencies of the Kings of Mercia.

Actually, Hertfordshire was once reckoned to be one of the healthiest locations in the British Isles. This was due to the high *oxygen* content given off by the huge population of *trees*.

It just goes to show that, even back in the 16th and 17th centuries, Mankind was aware of the debt he owes to trees.

Our forebears it seems, had an inherent awareness of the balance of nature, which we sadly seem to have lost during the course of the Twentieth Century!

During my 30-year career as a gardener, particularly when working for municipal bodies, I have had many people complaining whilst I and my colleagues were planting roadside trees in built-up areas.

They have complained that the tree will 'block out Sunlight', or 'The leaves will get *everywhere*'!

When I have tried to explain to them that the trees will actually *help to keep them alive*, they have looked at me as though I were some kind of *madman*!

ALAS! Where there were once massive forests and delicate woodland, there now sprawls new towns, housing estates and motorways!

Other great forests such as those at Epping, and Sherwood, the legendary home of Robin Hood, are gradually being eaten away by urban development. All this for the glorification of the motor-car.

With it has gone much of the wildlife too! Wolves and wild boar roamed Sherwood Forest in the days of Robin Hood. Now these creatures are totally extinct in Britain. *Other* woodland creatures are rapidly approaching the same fate.

Of course, the past is merely a rudder by which we may steer ourselves correctly towards the future. Our future *MUST* be to preserve our natural heritage. Not just in Britain, but throughout the world.

Much has been made of the destruction of the tropical rain forests, particularly in Brazil. However, *EVERY* country must do it's bit towards re—planting the Earth's garden, before it's too late!

Here in Britain, National Tree Planting year was launched in 1973, with the brave slogan, PLANT A TREE IN '73. Unfortunately, due to public and municipal *apathy*, it didn't have the effect intended.

It was hoped that municipal bodies would take up the challenge and plant not only *trees,* but whole *copses, woodlands,* and even *forests,* on any available site.

Many said that this was impracticable and uneconomic. Yet when the very *FUTURE OF THE PLANET* depends upon our actions. What could be more important?

The businessman would ask why he should turn over a plot of land to nature, when he could make a fortune out of it with industrial or civil development.

It is true that human beings are breeding faster every year. At the same time, we *live longer.*

In 1650 AD, the world population was estimated to be about 500 million. By 1950, it had risen to 2.5 million. By 1990, it had risen to 5.3 billion!

This means that more and more people are using more and more *oxygen*. Unfortunately, in our modern society, this means more *cars, buses, lorries* and *trains,* which burn more and more oxygen. 300 times more than Mankind himself. as we have already discussed.

More and more people need to keep warm in the winter, so more and more *fossil fuels* are plundered from the Earth. This in turn is *burned*, using up even *more* of our precious Oxygen.

On average, every human being uses up to *five times more oxygen than any other animal of the same size,* due to his *'civilized'* activities!

Industry and motor vehicles replace this with deadly gases such as sulphur dioxide, nitrous oxides and carbon monoxide.

Since our planet earth is surrounded by a near-vacuum of *space,* where does all this essential Oxygen *come from?*

It comes solely from *plant life,* and from the *waters of the earth,* as the power of the sun evaporates it, releasing it's oxygen and hydrogen molecules into the atmosphere. Animals and plants are natural *partners* in the business of keeping earth habitable. *Without each other, all life on Earth would cease to exist.*

Likewise, all the *pollutants* being pumped into the earth's atmosphere has *nowhere else* to go but to *remain in the atmosphere.*

Once there, it continues to poison the earth, just like our examples of people, trees and motor cars in the glass dome. Obviously, being worldwide, this is on a much larger scale, so that if everything dies in a matter of months in our glass dome, so will life on earth die within two or three hundred years at the present rate!

So what effect did our *National Tree Planting* year have on the environment in 1973?

Ironically, we failed to check the infamous Dutch Elm Disease (DED) which swept the country in that very year.

In *some* cases, acres of woodland were ripped up for *urban development!* Whole acres of trees were demolished to make way for new roads and motorways.

True, many local authorities did their *best* to plant trees, as did many ordinary people. For all those official and unofficial conservationists however, there were dozens *more* official and unofficial *vandals*!

Much concern was expressed in that year, about the menace of Dutch Elm Disease, yet *STILL* the disease continued to spread. This was despite the fact that many *healthy* trees could have been isolated from the *infected* ones, simply by digging *trenches* around them!

This action would have prevented infected roots from coming into contact with healthy ones.

It was *also* possible to introduce a *small wasp* which feeds upon the carrier of the disease, *ring bark beetle*.

It is very likely that the use of *insecticides* killed off many of these wasps, leaving the ring bark beetle to run rampant!

Similar examples have happened in previous and subsequent years, with greenfly and *other* aphids.

Insecticides have killed off thousands of ladybirds (the natural predator of the aphids) leaving the so-called 'garden pests' to have a field day on our garden plants!

So it is quite possible that *man himself* was the cause of the Dutch Elm Disease plague of the early seventies!

Left alone *without* Mankind's intervention via the use of chemicals, nature *will* keep the balance. The sooner Mankind learns to leave well alone the better!

Unfortunately, this will never happen, until the gardener *disregards the propaganda pumped out by the chemicals Industry,* and begins to work *with* nature, rather than *against* it!

Even the mighty *oak*, that symbol of Britain might and the heart of many an ancient ship, has been toppling over during the past few years.

This is due to one weakness. Not the ring bark beetle. Not even the *polluted* atmosphere, but by the *disturbance of it's roots!*

Many authorities have slapped preservation orders on these majestic trees. Builders, against their natural instincts (or should I say *unnatural* instincts !) have had to build *around* them.

Sadly, in some cases, they have disturbed their roots.

The mighty oak, able to withstand hurricanes, storms, and even heavy vehicles smashing into them, is dying. With it goes not only a part of our *national heritage*, but also one of our essential partners in the game of life. The teeming life which exists in its branches and in its bark *also* perishes.

Mankind has been tipping the scales in the wrong direction for so many years now that it is almost too late to regain the balance.

This is exactly what we *MUST* try to do though, *BEFORE IT IS TOO LATE!*

Chapter Six

THE PAVEMENTS ARE GROWING

EXTREMELY WELL

Readers of this book who are old enough, may well remember the countryside as it was in the 1940s, before the development of the new towns and motorways.

In those days, we could travel out into the counryside for a little peace and quiet. We could get away from the noise of the city and the fumes of the traffic (such as it was then!)

The good news is that there are still a few isolated places left in Britain. The bad news is that they are rapidly becoming much rarer!

Even those that do exist don't fully escape the scourge of pollution and the indignity of being robbed of their natural flora by nature-starved townsfolk.

Back in those halcyon days during the springtime, cowslips grew abundantly in the meadows. They were known to countryfolk as *paigles* or *peggles*, meaning 'golden keys' because of the way the golden-yellow flowers hung in bunches from the stems.

The woods were a living picture of primroses and bluebells. Wood anemones, celandines and wood violets added to the picture.

Summer brought us fields of wild grasses scattered with buttercups, daisies, poppies and a host of *other* wild meadow flowers.

Stately trees were draped in their green summer clothes, whilst the fields were alive with rabbits, hares and fieldmice, birds and butterflies.

These all played happily amongst the flowers of nature's garden.

Now, where there once were green fields and trees, there are now pavements and roads.

Where the blackbirds once sang, now the motor-car speeds on it's way, poisoning all in it's wake.

'Concrete Jungle'

Even the traditional British pastime of picking wild fruit from the hedgerows is now a dangerous affair. The chances are that if you eat the fruit from nature's harvest, you will be *poisoned!*

Blackberries and other wild fruit, and even wild mushrooms growing near busy roads will almost certainly be coated with a deadly layer of lead from the exhausts of traffic. One survey shows that blackberries growing by the roadside can have as much as *FIVE TIMES THE ' SAFE ' LIMIT OF LEAD IN THEM!*

Personally, I don't think there is any *'safe'* limit for the consumption of lead, but then I refuse to accept many so-called 'safe' limits that the so-called 'experts' tell us!

To me, 'safe' limits is merely a cop-out, giving us a licence to carry on *polluting!*

Unfortunately, even fruit picked *further out* in the countryside may not be safe to eat either. If they are growing near the boundaries of a *farmers' field,* they could well be contaminated with chemicals from the 'drift' of a farmer's lethal sprays!

The British countryside is certainly not the idyllic haven it *used* to be!

COLCHICINE
FROM
COLCHICUM
AUTUMNALE

:aa867

During his comparatively short existence upon the earth, Mankind has discovered many of nature's secrets.

He is capable of using plants to produce drugs in combatting disease. He has learned to domesticate animals and foretell weather conditions. He has even learned to produce artificial foodstuffs, and to travel into space. These may, at first, seem like great achievements.

However, a *new* realisation is needed *urgently* by Mankind. The realisation that he cannot live out his life in defiance of the planet's complex mechanism.

Let's face it. For all Mankind's ingenuity, he has done *NOTHING* which nature hasn't already achieved. In fact usually, nature's originals do the job much more *efficiently*! The *aeroplane* is merely Mankind's puny attempt to fly like the birds, the bats, and even the pterodactyls long before *that*!

The camera is merely a copy of the eye. In fact, Mankind is *STILL* trying to work out how nature manages to get binocular three-dimensional images!

Electricity and radio waves have been there all the time. Mankind has only recently learned how to *use* them!

Meteorites have been travelling through the Galaxy long before Mankind discovered space travel. Indeed, they were doing this before even the *earth itself was formed! AND NATURE HAS DONE ALL THESE THINGS WITHOUT UPSETTING THE BALANCE!*

Unfortunately, most of us have been brainwashed by the hype

put out by *wealthy man* in an effort to make him even *wealthier!*.

From the family man who spends his Sundays washing his mechanical idol and spraying weedkiller on his paths and insecticide on his roses, the town planners, who can think only in terms of concrete and clay, to the building contractors, who rip up the countryside.

Most of us are guilty of destroying what is our only home in the universe.

THE PAVEMENTS ARE GROWING EXTREMELY WELL, BUT THIS IS TO THE DETRIMENT OF THE PLANTS WHICH GIVE US OUR LIFE-GIVING OXYGEN!

Shouldn't we be *changing* all this?

Shouldn't we be putting the horse before the cart and make *REAL* progress, in order to keep ourselves and our fellow life forms alive and healthy?

Trees should come before *flyovers, shrubs* before *roads, grass* before *pavements, nature's creatures* before *motor cars.*

After all, the internal-combustion engine *itself* will eventually become extinct, as the earth's supply of oil, formed over many millions of years, eventually dries up through Man's insatiable greed.

Shouldn't we be *helping* the countryside to grow well, instead of stifling it out of existence altogether?

Fortunately, there are *still* some remnants of nature's garden left to us. It is up to us to *maintain* them.

Some *wild orchids* still remain on the chalk hills of the Chilterns, although the greatest proportion of the colony have perished to make way for roads since the 1970s. The most beautiful of *all* wild British orchids, the lady's slipper orchid, *Cyprepedium calceolus*, is now thought to be virtually *extinct* in this country. It's final stronghold was in Northamptonshire.

The pasque flower, *pulsatilla vulgaris*, still makes a brave appearance in Bedfordshire, although they are now disappearing at an alarming rate. Again, this is totally due to roadworks and greedy plant collectors.

The very rare and beautiful oxlip *primula elatior* (pictured right) used to grow thick in the dark forests of Shakespeare's England. Indeed, they were mentioned in several of his works. Now however, they are battling for survival in East Anglia in just *five woods!*

There were *six* until 1972. In that year, I witnessed, to my horror, the destruction of this woodland, which happened to be in the middle of a farmer's land.

The fact that he was destroying one of the rarest plants in Britain didn't even *occur* to him. It was *his* land, and he *needed* it in order to make more *profit!*

I literally grabbed a few plants from the jaws of the bulldozer, and transferred them to my own garden, which was an official wildlife garden, registered by the Royal Society for Nature Conservation.

Oddly enough, in 1988, a *red* oxlip appeared in the middle of the normal yellow-flowered plants. Red oxlips are extremely rare, and I like to think this was nature's way of repaying me!

Primroses and bluebells were the favourites of children in days gone by, but now the habitats of these once very common plants are rapidly disappearing.

The oxlip mentioned previously, is certainly a plant worth protecting, as it is thought to be Britain's oldest existing primula, being the forerunner of both the primrose and the cowlip.

It is also one of the parents of the Victorian gold-laced polyanthus. This lovely little plant displays it's sulphur-coloured bell-shaped flowers in April, giving off a strong almond scent.

There was real fear amongst conservationists that the oxlip would become extinct by the end of this century. Fortunately, the five remaining woods where they grow are now protected by law.

Of course, the loss of so many of our British wild plants isn't *ALL* the blame of the civil engineers, town planners or the motor car, although these account for the *majority* of causes!

Ordinary people visiting the countryside can do *untold* damage, by digging up wild plants for their gardens.

The Oxlips which I saved in 1972 were definitely the *exception,* for without my intervention, they would have been destroyed. I was able to reproduce a natural environment for them. In fact, digging up wild plants is *illegal.*

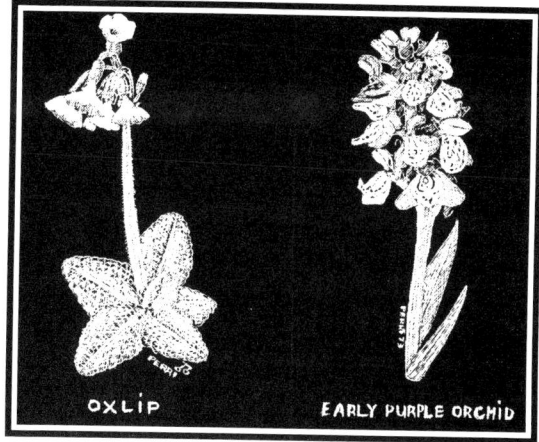

OXLIP   EARLY PURPLE ORCHID

It's a pity this law doesn't apply to civil engineers! Maybe one day, someone will bring forward a test case, to *question* this anomaly!

Many people have the idea 'one little root won't be missed', but the fact remains that *MANY* people taking 'just one little root' can have a devastating effect upon the colony.

Of course, these 'plantnappers' are not criminals in the *accepted* sense, even though I call the practice 'Robbery with violets'! They are merely keen amateur gardeners. Nevertheless, it is a fact that what they are doing *IS* a crime, *punishable by law!*

Many people assume that a plant growing in the wild is an easy subject to grow in the garden. This is far from true!

Every wild plant requires a different environment. *Garden* plants have been developed especially to suit *garden conditions.*

Primroses growing in a wood or by the bank of a stream grow there because conditions *suit them.* This is why various plants have their own 'territory'.

Take a primrose away from the damp leafy conditions of the woodland or stream bank and transplant it to a hot dry border where leaves are regularly cleared away to make the border look 'tidy', and the plants will wither away during the first season.

Violets, wood sorrel, bluebells and foxgloves require the same conditions as primroses, and will suffer the same fate if transplanted to the garden. *Garden* versions of these plants bought from a nursery or garden centre have been especially bred to *deal* with garden conditions. It is like capturing a wild bird and putting it in a cage. It will not survive.

I must admit that many of our native plants are very desirable, and *deserve* a place in our gardens. Indeed, I was one of the first garden journalists to advocate *wildlife gardening* in the sixties.

If you really *do* wish to bring a little bit of the countryside into your own domain, then buy specially cultivated specimens from a specialist nurseryman, or try collecting *SEEDS* from growing plants when the seed pods are ripe.

The plants will adapt more readily to garden conditions if they are raised from seed, and this practice is legal, except in the case of a few extremely rare species, such as the Lady's Slipper orchid, *Cypripedium calceoslous* (see picture) and other rare British orchids. It is worth checking this out first.

Please take the trouble to find out as much about the plants' natural habitat as possible, and try to recreate this in your garden. *This* way you could help to preserve some of our native wildlife.

CYPRIPEDIUM CALCEOLUS

Other plants which have become almost extinct in Britain include the snakeshead fritillary, *fritillaria meleagris* , which used to have the quaint country name of guinea flower, and the snowflakes, *leucojum aestivum* and *l. vernum*. The latter is known as the *Loddon lily*, as one of it's last strongholds is by the bank of the River Loddon.

Both of these plants can be brought as cultivated

plants from bulb merchants very cheaply, so it is certainly worth leaving those natural colonies still in existence strictly alone.

Another reason why plants should be left alone in the wild is the fact that each habitat has it's own Eco-system, where not only are soil conditions perfect for a certain colony of plants, but the balance of insects and micro-organisms is also prefect keeping pests and diseases to a minimum.

In the garden, this is rarely the case...

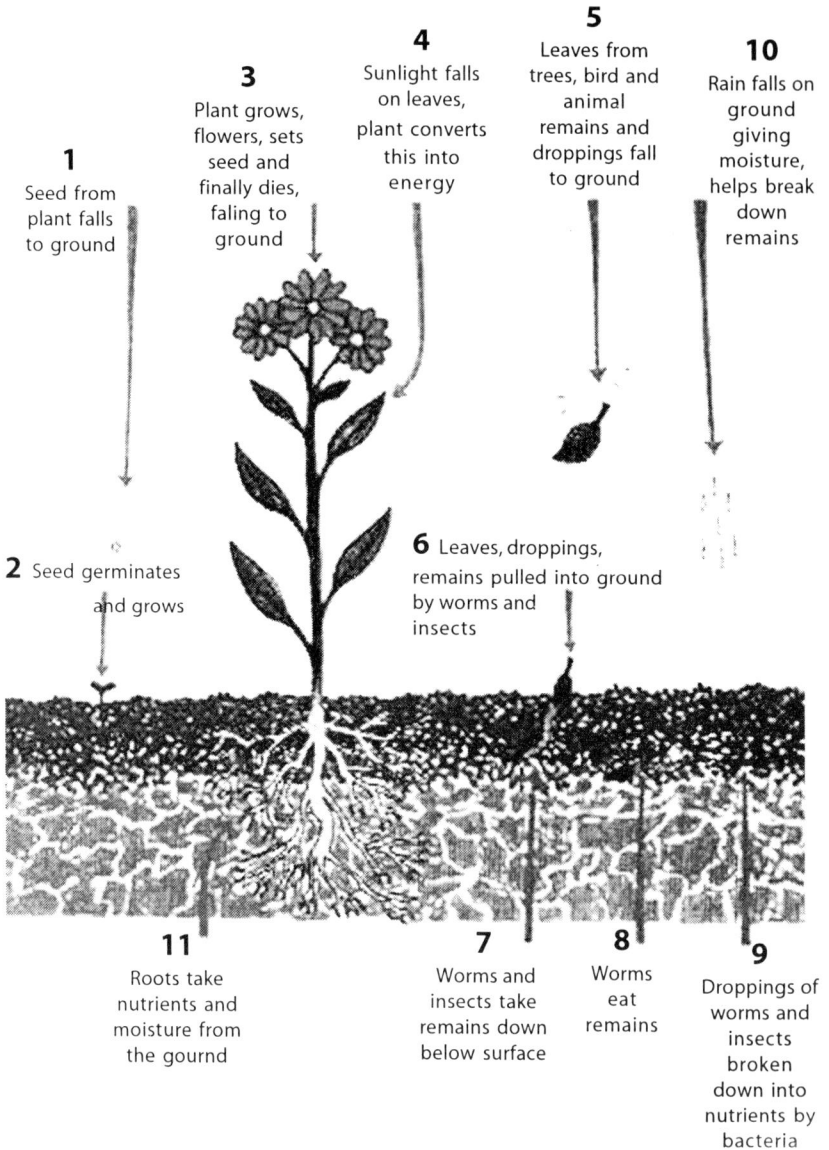

5
Leaves from trees, bird and animal remains and droppings fall to ground

4
Sunlight falls on leaves, plant converts this into energy

10
Rain falls on ground giving moisture, helps break down remains

3
Plant grows, flowers, sets seed and finally dies, faling to ground

1
Seed from plant falls to ground

2 Seed germinates and grows

6 Leaves, droppings, remains pulled into ground by worms and insects

11
Roots take nutrients and moisture from the gournd

7
Worms and insects take remains down below surface

8
Worms eat remains

9
Droppings of worms and insects broken down into nutrients by bacteria

Nature's Way

Chapter Seven

CHEMICAL WELFARE

OR CHEMICAL WARFARE?

It is a fact that plants in our homes and gardens are rapidly becoming 'hooked' on chemical fertilizers! We are doing untold damage to the balance of nature with the so-called 'labour-saving' weedkillers and pesticides.

Let us look firstly at the *nitrogen cycle*, which is the basis of how a plant in it's natural habitat gains nourishment and energy for it's growth and life.

Briefly, a plant grows from a seed, reaches maturity, sets seed again, and ultimately dies.

The *carcass* of the plant, together with the dead leaves from trees, the droppings of wild animals and birds, together with *their* dead carcasses, are taken into the soil by earth-worms. This material is then worked upon by various bacteria which, in turn, break down the raw materials into essential nutrients for immediate use by plants. The seed from the dead plants germinate, grow-ing and maturing, by feeding on the chemicals produced by the bacteria from the remnants of material in the soil. So it goes on, generation after generation. In nature, there is *no such thing* as *waste*!

Most *CHEMICAL FERTILIZERS* certainly contain the essential plant foods, *carbon, hydrogen, oxygen, nitrogen, sulphur, phosphorus, potassium, calcium, magnesium* and *iron*. They also contain vital *trace elements*, so that the plant *CAN* survive in a totally lifeless compost which contains a good chemical fertilizer. *That* however, is only in the *SHORT* term. In the *LONG* term, it can have disastrous effects on the very *life of the planet!*

Let us assume that we grow all our plants in this lifeless compost, feeding them solely on chemical fertilizer.

We neatly remove all the dead and dying flowers and leaves from the plant, as many gardeners do with garden flowers. This ensures that the compost remains almost sterile.

Now suppose we extend this practice to the garden, clearing away all the natural litter in the way of leaves and garden debris. *WHAT WOULD THE EARTHWORMS FEED ON?*

There would be no *humus* in the soil, but then there wouldn't be any *need* for the earthworms anyway, as they wouldn't have any work to do! They wouldn't have anything to *eat,* either! As a result, there would be no leaves, droppings or carcasses in the soil. There would be no need for those bacteria, as the chemicals would already be there in *artificial* form! These would be of no use to the bacteria, so ultimately, earthworms and garden insects would perish through lack of food. This would cause the extinction of the bacteria.

The constant use of chemicals would mean that there would be no 'bulk' in the soil, and no life whatsoever. Therefore, there would be nothing to hold the soil particles *together.* Consequently, our once-fertile soil would be reduced to nothing more than dust!

No doubt we would carry on regardless, believing that as long as our plants get water and the essential elements, why should we worry about the teeming life in *natural* soil? Such nonchalance is highly *dangerous* however! Man has yet to learn that he cannot be totally independent of the *other* forms of life on this planet.

Thousands of years ago, man grew corn in Egypt. He discovered how to cultivate it and how to reap it, but he did not understand that he had to put something back into the soil.

The result of that lack of understanding is the great deserts we know today.

If there are no *earthworms* and *insects* in the soil, *birds* will abandon the area, because they *rely* on these creatures for food. *Fish* too, would soon starve for the same reason. Dead birds on the land and dead fish in the sea, without bacteria to break them down, would pollute the land and the waters. Animal's drinking water would become contaminated, and *they* would die. This would add to the piles of dead bodies. At *this* rate, earth would soon become a dead planet.

The same kind of thing applies to *insecticides*. *Ladybirds* feed on *greenfly* and *other* aphids. The balance of nature has been perfected throughout millions of years. A long time before *Mankind* made an appearance upon this planet! Man then invented an *insecticide* in order to get rid of the greenfly, which he regards as a 'pest'.

Naturally, this insecticide also kills the greenfly's predator, the *ladybird*, so the ratio between *greenfly* and *ladybird* remains unchanged, even though the *numbers* of both species have been drastically depleted.

The problem is that by *killing* these insects, we are robbing *birds* of their food! We use insecticides in our homes, spraying flies, moths, bees and wasps. As a result, *plants* suffer, because there are not enough *pollinators* left to keep the populations of the plants going!

We have already discussed how a *particular* species of wasp could have been reduced in numbers due to the use of sprays, leaving the *ring bark beetle* to spread the Dutch Elm Disease in the Seventies.

Even the killing of *flies* (which many people regard as useless insects) can have disastrous effects. Some plants notably from the *arum* family, rely *solely* upon flies, to pollinate them! This will be discussed more fully in a *later chapter*.

Why can't we accept the fact that *spiders* are *much* more efficient at catching flies than any household or garden spray? The sad fact is that by *using* these sprays, we are killing the *spiders too*!

We now know too, that the *CFCs* in *spray cans* are helping to destroy the earth's protective *ozone layer*, so that *ALL* life on earth is at risk! What we *must* remember is that every living creature on this planet has a *purpose* in life.

ALL life, whether it be *animal insect, plant,* and even *viruses and bacteria,* must be respected, and allowed to carry out their natural functions.

If we succeed in killing *all insect life* (and this is quite possible) with millions of people using insecticides every day, none of our *flowering plants* could reproduce. All of our *wild flowers* would die out as all the old plants died of old age. There would be no *seedlings* to take their places! *Cereal crops* and *fruit* would become extinct too, and many plants which we use for medicines, and 'economic' plants such as *cotton, linen, rice, cocoa, coffee, tea*, etc., would all be gone!

In fact *every* plant you can *think of* would die out, apart from the few trees which are wind-pollinated, and those plants which have alternative methods of fertilization. This will be discussed in a later chapter.

Weedkillers too, are a distinct threat to nature, especially on the scale it is used today. Killing 'weeds' may make a garden look neat and tidy, but at the same time, it ruins the soil by taking away the fibre, made up of plant roots, which are just as essential as the humus in the soil, for holding the ground together.

After the great British hurricanes of 1987, there was so much damage to woodland, that the Forestry Commission decided to replant only *half* of the damaged woodland. The rest was left to nature. Ten years on, they discovered that many of the new saplings replanted on the ground that had been cleaned up had died. The parts which had been left to *nature* however, had regenerated itself much more efficiently! There is a lesson here which most *definitely* should be learned!

Many plants regarded by Mankind as 'weeds' are essential *food* for many *other* forms of life. Many butterflies lay their eggs on *stinging nettles*. The hatching caterpillars need the leaves to *eat*, whilst many *birds* need those same caterpillars for *food*. The *IMMEDIATE* effects of these chemicals isn't the *only* problem however.

Many weedkillers stay in the soil for many years, rendering that piece of ground useless. Even those said to become neutralized once in contact with the soil have lasting effects contrary to what the manufacturers tell us.

Many plots of land that have been sprayed with so-called 'safe' weedkillers such as Diquat and paraquat, will grow, after treatment, nothing but moss. This shows that the treated piece f land has become 'stale', and too *acid* for most forms of plant life.

Remember too, that these weedkilllers are *not* safe if consumed by *children or animals*! Weedkillers also have a nasty habit of seeping through the soil into the water table, which eventually finds it's way to the rivers and the sea, where it can kill fish and water creatures, as well as water plants. This begins a continuous chain reaction which affects all life on the planet!

MAN HAS THE ABILITY TO *REASON* AND TO *UNDERSTAND* THESE PROBLEMS, BUT DOES HE REALLY KNOW ENOUGH ABOUT THE WORLD AROUND HIM?

CAN HE *REALLY* UNDERSTAND HIS FELLOW INHABITANTS OF THE PLANET EARTH, AND CAN HE OVERTURN HIS GREED FOR WEALTH IN FAVOUR OF WORKING *WITH* NATURE, INSTEAD OF *AGAINST* IT?

CAN MAN *REALLY* UNDERSTAND THE PLANT LIFE OF THIS GARDEN EARTH, UPON WHICH IS HE SO UNDOUBTEDLY DEPENDENT?

PART THREE

PLANTS MAY NOT LAUGH & CRY
BUT THEY ARE SO SENSITIVE !

Chapter Eight

MOVEMENT AND SENSITIVITY

Some people think of plants as inanimate objects, put on the earth for the sole pleasure of man, whilst others believe that they are only good for eating, and for making medicines, drugs, oil and rubber.

There is, however, a third school of thought to which I strongly subscribe.

Plants are living, thinking inhabitants of the earth, which deserve as much help and consideration as man or beast! After all, plant life started on Earth two thousand million years before Man took his first tentative steps upon the planet. How then could it have been put there solely for his exclusive use?

A man may laugh when he is happy and cry when he is sad. A dog will wag his tail with pleasure, and growl in fear and anger. These things may easily be understood by Mankind, for we are all a part of the Animal Kingdom, but plants are *different*.

They are the oldest inhabitants of the Earth. They can neither laugh nor cry, growl nor whimper, so how can we possibly understand the *'emotions'* of plants? Let us now venture into the wonderful world of plants, into their *private lives*. How do they react to the elements around them and beneath them? How do they fit into life's general pattern, and how do they struggle for survival against the terrific odds that face them, as did their forbears all those millions of years ago?

Let us *watch* them and *touch* them, *work* with them and *play* with them. Let us learn to *understand* that *plants have feeling too!* Although plants cannot walk from place to place as *we* do, they can certainly *move* in many ingenious ways.

When the seed of any plant *germinates,* it sends out it's *RADICLE,* or *seedling root*, and it's *PLUMULE* or *seedling shoot*. The plumule ventures *upwards* towards the light, whilst the radicle moves *downwards* into the soil.

This tells us that plants are sensitive to the law of gravity. This sensitivity is known scientifically as *GEOTROPISM.*

Geotropism can be illustrated in adult plants in many ways, one way being when a potted plant is turned on it's side. Note that, after a few hours, the plant will attempt to straighten itself up, so that the main stem will be pointing straight upwards, regardless of the angle of the pot.

Another example of geotropism is in the fact that a tree growing on the side of a hill will always grow up vertically from the *centre of the earth*, rather than to the level of the *soil surrounding it.*

As any gardener will know, plants are also highly sensitive to *light*. This can be observed when a house plant is not *turned* regularly. The stem and the leaves will always turn themselves towards the *light source*. This action is known scientifically as *PHOTOTROPISM.*

The *purpose* of phototropism is to ensure that the leaves are placed in such a way as to make full use of whatever light is available. This allows the plant to *PHOTOSYNTHESIZE,* or turn Sunlight into energy. This sensitivity to light can be illustrated by observing two identical plants, one growing in *direct sunlight*, and the other growing in a *shaded* position.

The one growing in *full Sunlight* will be sturdy and of a good strong green colouring. The *shaded* specimen will be long and drawn, and of an insipid yellowish colour.

The reason why the shaded plant becomes long and drawn is because it is reaching out in search of energy-giving light. The lack of light is also shown in the pallid colour of the leaves.

Remember in part one of the book, how we showed that Mankind *himself* needed sunlight for it's vitamin C content? His skin became paler, allowing more Sunlight to enter it.

If a *plant* does not find sufficient light, it will eventually 'outgrow it's strength' and die.

However, because ours is a planet of light and shade, some plants, notably *woodland plants* and those which grow in dense jungles, have adapted themselves to make maximum use of minimum light. This is why a plant like our native woodland primrose will not survive in a sun-baked border!

These examples show that plants have the power to adapt themselves to various environmental conditions, in an effort to follow certain laws laid down by nature in the same ways that animals, including humans, must follow certain natural laws in order to survive.

Let us take a look at some individual plants, and how they react to environmental changes and outside stimuli, in order to reach various objectives.

The *first* plant to spring to mind when discussing the sensitivity of plants is *mimosa pudica,* also known as the 'sensitive plant'.

This plant is sensitive to *touch* (HAPTOTROPISM), and changes in *light intensity* (photonasty). If the leaves of the mimosa are *touched*, they will droop and fold up. The same thing happens if you *knock* the plant, or even the *pot in which it is growing*. It also happens if you blow *smoke* at it, as my pal *Les* did in our opening story! This plant also folds up it's leaves during periods of *darkness,* as though it were going to *sleep!*

Other plants sensitive in this way to air currents and degrees of light, are our native wood sorrel, *oxalis acetocella,* the wood anemone, *anemone nemorosa,* clovers, and the common field daisy, *bellis perrenis.*

The flowers of these plants *ALSO* close up at night. This is thought to prevent night-flying insects from pollinating them, for reasons which I will explain in a later chapter. The reason why plants fold their leaves up in *windy weather* is to reduce the loss of moisture through the leaves. In *most* plants, flowers open wider in *sunny weather*, as with tulips and crocuses. This is so that the flowers are more noticeable and more accessible to pollinating insects, which are likely to be more abundant during warm sunny spells.

Bellis Perrenis (daisy)

Crocus

Plants which open their flowers wider in warm weather are sensitive to changes in *temperature*, rather than the concentration of *light*. This is known as *THERMONASTY*.

The Telegraph plant, *desmodium motorium*, (syn. *d.gyrans*), is a plant which is sensitive to heat in a rather *different* way.

This is the plant which my pal *Les* was so fascinated by, when it appeared to 'fan' itself when I directed the fan heater towards it.

When the temperature exceeds 22°C (72°F), the leaflets of this plant start moving in all directions.

This is an effort by the plant to keep it's leaves cool, reducing the drying effect on the leaves in high temperatures.

In *this* plant *too*, the leaves fold up at night.

Perhaps the most interesting examples of movement and sensitivity are to be found in the *insectivorous plants*, most of which grow in moist peat, or boggy conditions, which are deficient in that most essential element for plant growth *nitrogen*.

Again, as I showed Les in our opening story, these plants lure and trap insects and small animals, extracting essential nitrogen and *other* minerals from their bodies.

The Venus Fly Trap, *dionea muscipula*, has such a high degree of sensitivity that it has been compared with a primitive *nervous system*. When an insect settles on the lobes of the plant, there is an immediate reflex action, causing the lobes to close together, trapping the insect within.

These lobes are modified *leaves*, which *also* act in the *normal* way of helping the plant to breathe, transpire excess moisture, and to photosynthesize. They are so *specialized* though, that they even have a row of *barbs* around the edge of the lobes, like little *fangs*.

When closed together, these make a very effective 'cage' in which to ensnare their 'prey'.

Other insectivorous plants include the *sundews*, which ensnares their prey with sticky tentacles on the leaves. The *sarracenias*, have long *horn-shaped* leaves with a sticky liquid in the base and slippery sides. This makes it impossible for any non-flying insect or even a small *amphibian*, to escape.

There are also the *pitcher plants*, which act in a similar way. The *bladderworts* are a race of *water* plants, which trap water-loving insects, and even small fish and tadpoles.

Finally, there are the *sea anemones*. These however, are not *true plants*, but plant-like *animals*.

Yet another form of movement displayed by plants is known as *AUTONOMIC MOVEMENT.*

This is noted particularly in climbing plants such as *peas, passion flowers* and *clematis*. In these plants, the *tendrils* (specially adapted prehensile leaves) grow in an upward direction, describing a circular movement. When these tendrils come into contact with an object to which it can cling, it wraps itself around it.

It is interesting to note that most plant tendrils in the *northern hemisphere* go in a *clockwise* direction, whereas those in the *southern hemisphere* go in an *anti-clockwise* direction. This is believed to occur because the plant is influenced by the earth's *rotation*.

This also occurs when water goes down a plughole on opposite sides of the earth. In *Europe*, for example, water drains away in a *clockwise* direction, whereas in *Australasia*, it drains away in an *anti-clockwise* direction!

It has even been claimed that in those countries which break nature's rule by driving cars on the *right-hand* side of the road in the *northern* hemisphere, (going *anti*-clockwise round a roundabout), and on the *left-hand* side in the *southern* hemisphere (*clockwise* round the roundabouts) more tornados occur. This is because we are driving contrary to the earth's rotation. It is claimed that this anti-natural practice actually 'winds up' tornados!

But back to the *plants*!

So far, we have shown that, although plants cannot *see* in the sense that we mere *humans* can understand, they can most certainly react to *touch*, and are fully aware of their own needs for survival against the hazards surrounding them.

We may find it difficult to comprehend how any living thing can detect light without being able to *see it with eyes*. Plants *can* do this however!

We may *also* find it difficult to understand how it is possible to detect the pull of earth's gravity without jumping *up and down*, or *dropping something*. Plants can *certainly* manage it!

We can understand the fact that we shiver when we get *cold*, and that animals and babies *curl up* in order to keep themselves *warm*.

We are *amazed*, however, when we see plants folding themselves up in *cold* weather, or fanning themselves when it is too *hot*! We also find it curious that a plant is capable of luring and trapping *other* forms of life for nourishment, yet we take it for granted when this applies to *animals and humans!*

We find it incomprehensible that a plant can detect the earth's rotation, as they undoubtedly do with autonomic movement. *We* have no way of detecting this, apart from watching water drain away down a plughole! Perhaps, due to civilization, we have *lost* the ability!

Aren't plants entitled to just as much right, if not more, to be on this planet as any *other* life form?

They were, after all, the very first organisms to *populate* the planet!

We humans fight for survival in what we regard as a hostile world. We are fascinated at stories of survival among wild animals. *Plants* however, have to put up with conditions in which we would find it *impossible* to survive!

They are struggling for survival more *now*, that at any *other* time in the history of this planet.

Plants struggle for survival in much more subtle ways than those applied by humans and other animals ...

Chapter Nine

SURVIVAL AND REPRODUCTION

If people were *shot* every time the Government wanted to purchase their land for building, there would be a major revolution in this country.

If *animals* are exterminated for the same reason, there is public outcry. Very few people, however, concern themselves with the mass destruction of *plants* and *trees* for such projects, and yet they are as much a part of this earth as any human or animal. Why then, do they not command as much *respect?*

Probably because they cannot run for cover in the sense that we can understand, and they do not fight back in the way *we* do.

Plants are nature's *pacifists*, and like their human counterparts throughout the ages, they are bullied and destroyed by the most violent and selfish creatures ever to exist on this Garden Earth, *Human Beings …*

If a tree could cry, or hit back as an axe struck into it's flesh, then maybe people would feel different. So far unfortunately, they haven't *evolved* these abilities. In terms of evolution, Mankind hasn't been *around* long enough for the plants to *adapt.*

Plants are far from being *stupid*, as we have found in the previous chapter. They are *fully aware* of what is going on around them, and they know what a great threat Mankind is to their existence.

Instead of meeting violence with violence though, they find ways of carrying on with their lives, and of reproducing against all odds, even though Man is making life increasingly difficult for them.

Men take wild rootstocks and graft foreign plants on top of them (scions) in order to produce good garden plants as quickly, and with as much profit as possible. In so doing however, he very often puts the *original* plant (the rootstock) in *peril.*

Many modern pear trees are grafted on to the rootstock of the wild pear or, more commonly, the wild quince. The demand for these fruit trees has been so great, that the original wild plants are in danger of becoming totally *extinct*.

The gardener may get annoyed with the annual task of having to cut away the 'suckers' from his cultivated fruit trees and roses, but how many of us stop to think that the *original* plant, forced to play 'pick-a-back' to some man-produced hybrid, is only trying to grow in the way that nature *intended?*

Would *YOU* remain trapped underneath a foreign intruder if there was some chance of escape?

One of the most ingenious 'escape attempts' is illustrated by the wild *dog rose* stock, which is often made to act as host to our modern hybrid tea and floribunda roses. The plants begin to produce growth from below soil level, breaking to the surface close to the root.

The gardener regards these as '*suckers*', and cuts them off with secatuers, as close to the rootstock as possible. Does the plant *give up* on its escape attempt? *OF COURSE NOT!*

The following season, the plant sends out *more* 'suckers', breaking the surface of the soil further away form the rootstock. This is in the hope that it will go undetected. Unfortunately for the plant, the gardener *DOES* notice it! He promptly *cuts it off* again.

Year after year the same ritual take place, with suckers appearing *further and further* away from the original plant each time, until, as in some recorded cases, 'suckers' have ventured above ground some *six feet away from the original rootstock!* The gardener's small problem with 'suckering' is the plant's earnest attempt at *self-preservation !*

The humble lesser celandine, *ranunculus ficaria* is a prime example of self-preservation.

Back in the sixties when I was working for Blackpool (Lancs) Corporation, I was asked by the Parks Superintendent, Norman Leech, to create a woodland garden out of a wild, unkempt piece of scrubland. Growing abundantly on this land were the dainty buttercup-like plants of the lesser celandine.

I thought the plants looked pretty, but Mr. Leech told me to spray the whole area with paraquat weedkiller. Against my better judgment, I complied. Sure enough, the leaves and flowers shrivelled up and died. Come the following spring however, they were as abundant as ever!

Still my boss was insistent, so we rotovated the whole area. The result was that we scattered the little bulbils even further afield. The following spring, they returned even more abundant than *ever!*

The fact is that this little plant, like many other tuberous-rooted plants, is capable of storing energy in it's tubers and bulbils and remaining dormant until the threat of the weedkiller is gone. It simply *THRIVES* on being cut up into smaller pieces! It's just like taking cuttings, and will merely succeed in increasing the colony!

I eventually pointed out to my boss that when in flower, the plant DID look pretty, and many visitors commented favourably about them. Besides, soon after flowering, it loses its leaves *anyway!*

He agreed to leave it be, and that colony survives in the Blackpool woodland garden near Stanley Park to this day! I believe it adds to the beauty of the garden, growing, as it does, amongst the primulas and bluebells.

Thinking back, I often wonder why Norman Leech, a much loved and respected gardener and nature-lover of the time, wanted them *destroyed?*

Another example of a plant scorning any attempt to destroy it is to be found in the common yellow stonecrop *sedum acre*, which is *also* native to the British Isles. This plant can be chopped, literally, into *thousands of pieces*, and will respond by producing thousands of *new plants!* Birds actually help to *spread* the plant in this way, but more about that in the *next* chapter.

A Man chops down a tree at ground level, only to discover that, next season, there is a coppice of new branches sprouting up from on top of, and around the tree stump.

We must remember though, that not *ALL* plants have such resistance, and even the *strongest* armies may fall against *impossible odds*.

Plants do, however, have a survival kit which no human or animal can equal; the delayed-action seed! This was widely observed soon after the 'blitz' on London during World War Two.

Many people died because of Mankind's lust for power, and ancient buildings were flattened to the ground. No doubt many innocent *animals* perished too, as bombs left craters and bare soil, where, for hundreds of years, there had been roads and buildings

Within a few weeks of this carnage however, *plant seedlings* covered these areas, and within months, the bomb sites of London were ablaze with flowers.

Lady's Smock, Oxeye daisies, field buttercups, poppies, and many others, which were thought to be *extinct* in the region, Further investigations showed that many of these seeds had been laying dormant in the ground, covered by buildings and concrete, for hundreds of years. They had germinated as soon as the ground had been exposed to the elements once again. SO EVEN *BOMBS* CANNOT TOTALLY DESTROY PLANT LIFE!

I was only eight years old when the war finished, but I remember being enthralled by this show of defiance by nature.

The thing is, that, at the beginning of the war, I was evacuated with my mother and sisters to Fort George, in the Scottish Highlands, where my father was serving with the Seaforth Highlanders. From the age of two, I had grown to *love* the wild rugged countryside of the highlands.

For some unaccountable reason, we all returned to Walthamstow, East London, in the *middle of the Blitz!* Can you imagine the shock to my young nature, being taken from a peaceful country life to bombs and dogfights? No wonder I was so happy to see flowers growing in the dismal bomb sites of London!

The determination of plants to survive against all odds can *also* be seen in derelict areas, where mankind has abandoned his towns and cities.

Whilst working under contract for Brent (London) Council in the Seventies, I came across an old wartime 'pre-fab village', which had been left, totally abandoned by the council. The reason it had been left to go derelict for so long was because one old lady refused to leave her prefab. They couldn't pull it down, or build upon it until after she died.I took a walk around this 'ghost town' one lunchtime, and was amazed at nature's resilience.

Humble grasses and herbaceous plants had actually *LIFTED UP THE PAVING STONES AND THE TARMACKED ROADS, IN ORDER TO SEEK OUT THE LIGHT OF DAY!*

A TREE HAD GROWN IN AN OLD TELEPHONE BOX, LIFTING IT OFF THE GROUND, SO THAT THE TELEPHONE BOX WAS NOW PERCHED PRECARIOUSLY IN THE UPPERMOST BRANCHES!

Naturally, the force of the growth of the tree had long since snapped the cable which connected the telephone.

Ears of corn, found in an Egyptian tomb, estimated to be about 4,000 years old, were recently sown in seed trays in botanical gardens. They germinated within a few weeks !

On the basis of this discovery, scientists and botanists discussed the possibility of storing seeds of plants which are under threat of extinction, and re-introducing them long after the plant has officially become extinct. In fact, at Kew Gardens they have now started a 'seed bank' of plants from all over the world for this very purpose, so that extinct plants can be re-introduced when it is considered safe to do so.

It is a sad fact that many people do not *appreciate* something until it is *gone.*

Those bold scientists and botanists are patiently awaiting the day when the rest of Mankind comes to it's senses! It's heartening to know that there *are* some human beings who care about *this garden earth!*

Plants *also* adapt themselves to *NATURAL* hazards.

This is admirably displayed in the plant known as the Rose of Jericho, *anastaica hierochuntica*. This plant is also known as 'the resurrection plant', because, in dry arid weather, it completely withers, loosening itself from the soil, to form a loose ball shape.

DAY ONE

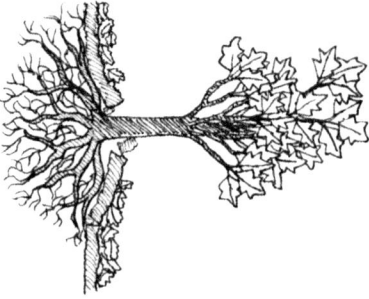

TWO YEARS

DAY SEVEN

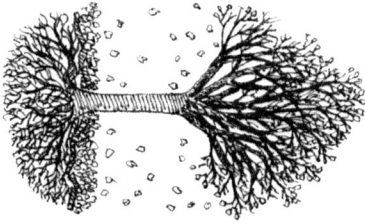

TEN YEARS

How a tiny seed can destroy a motorway!

3 WEEKS

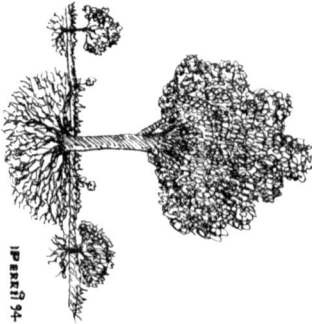

THIRTY YEARS

86

It is then blown about the desert like the *tumbleweed* of old Hollywood westerns, until the rainy season. Once the rain has soaked the earth, the plant opens out into a fern-like plant rooting itself into the now moist ground. It then flowers, and scatters it's seed into the ground around it. The seeds germinate and grow on, until the long hot dry season. When the dry season returns, the parent plant, together with the seedlings 'lift anchor' again to blow around the desert awaiting the next rainy season.

Rose of Jericho

So the cycle continues for this 'mobile plant', which never knows where it will be growing form one season to the next!

Actually, plants go to amazing lengths to reproduce themselves in order to perpetuate the species. In fact, they are probably far more aware of future events than *we* are!

When a *lupin* plant gets old and nearing the end of it's natural life, it will produce an abundance of flowers in an attempt to keep the species going.

Wood Violet

After the old plant dies, a host of seedlings appear around the dead plant. Old gardeners used to call this practice 'flowering itself to death'. In fact, the plant *KNEW* it was nearing the end of it's life, and was merely attempting to perpetuate itself.

This instinct for survival and reproduction has given rise to many ingenious mechanisms in

87

plants, such as the difference between true, and *cleistogamous* flowers in the *wood violet*.

We are all familiar with the true flowers of the violet, nodding in the spring breezes. Very often though, the weather at this early time of year is *too cold* for pollinating insects to venture out to do their work, especially in the uncertain climatic times in which live. Knowing this, the violet has devised an emergency mechanism, just in case the flowers do not become pollinated.

In the *summer* months, while the plant is making *leaves*, they produce small green insignificant flowers, known to scientists as *CLEISTOGOMOUS* flowers. These are *self-pollinating*.

Indeed, the flowers are so inconspicuous as to go completely unnoticed by the casual observer. However, they do their work in ensuring the reproduction of the species during these times of 'insect famine'!

These flowers don't *have* to be noticeable, because they don't have to attract any *insects*. They are *self-pollinating*.

Indeed, the only reason *why* flowers appear so colourful and attractive, and smell so sweet certainly isn't in order to give us humans a great deal of pleasure! It is to attract insects and other small creatures which carry out the act of *pollination*. In a way, I suppose it is a form of sexual allure!

Cross-pollination is *favoured* by plants, because it produces stronger offspring. *Self*-pollination, as in the *cleistogomous flowers* of the violet, is used *only* as an emergency device. Most *spring* flowers, you will notice, are particularly bright and colourful. Very often, they also have a *strong scent*. The *reason* for this is that there are comparatively few *insects* about during the early months of the year.

Flowers which open at *this* time of year need to attract the few insects which *are* around! It is also a fact that various insects are attracted by different *colours*, and different *scents*. This helps to prevent *crossbreeding* of *related species*.

Mankind, in his dubious wisdom, actually *encourages* this, purely for his own pleasure and convenience! Many flowers even have *guide-*

lines, designed to help insects find their way to the nectaries, which produces the *nectar*. This nectar is the 'bait' which attracts the actual pollination of the flowers. The sweet, high-energy substance is *essential* for the health of the insect.

Indeed, many *butterflies* feed on *nothing else*! This 'reward' is given to the insect for pollinating the flower! Yet *another* case of different species working together for the benefit of each other!

The 'guide-lines' are particularly noticeable in *wild* pansies (pictured), where they form distinct 'landing strips'.

Again, purely for his own satisfaction, mankind has developed these into 'blotches' in the larger *garden* pansies. To me, these huge great flowers are a travesty against nature!

It is quite likely that plants actually derive *pleasure* from fertilization, as *we* do from *sexual intercourse*! Pleasure is nature's *reward* to encourage *all* forms of life to reproduce and thrive. *Insects* enjoy the taste of nectar in the same way that *we* enjoy the taste of our food and drink.

It follows therefore, that *plants* enjoy sex in much the same way that *mankind* and the *animals* do! *Some* plants go to *incredible lengths* to ensure that they are fertilized. One of the most fascinating occurs in the *arums*.

Insects enter the *spathe* (the large hooded 'flower') of the arum to collect nectar. They literally have to *force* their way past the hair-like filaments inside. As these filaments grow in a *downward* direction however, the insects find themselves *trapped*, and unable to get back out.

In a frantic attempt to escape, the insects fly around, shaking the pollen onto the stigma, thus fertilizing the plant. The arum however, needs to ensure that the *fly species* survives, so that it can continue to help in the plant's reproduction.

With this in mind, plenty of nectar is provided for the insects in order to keep them alive. Once *fertilization* has taken place, the filaments within the spathe whither away, enabling the insects to escape. Mission accomplished!

Flies are *attracted* to the arums because they emit a strong *dung-like* smell. This happens to be *attractive* to flies, because they lay their *eggs* in dung and rotting matter. The smell, however, is *repulsive* to *other* creatures, including mankind!

This way ,the plant attracts *only* the creatures which are *useful* to it, and *repels* anything which might *damage* it. *The arums are masters at specialization*! Even *more* amazing tricks for the purpose of fertilization are used by members of the *orchid* family.

Their flowers actually mimic *insects, caterpillars,* and even *ducks!* In the orchids, a baby lays in a red cot, a ghost hangs eerily on a stem, and a duck traps an insect! All this merely to perpetuate the species!

Yes, there really *are* remarkable examples of mimicry in the world of orchids. Thought to be the most advanced of *all* plants, the orchids go to amazing lengths in their endless endeavor to spread their pollinia (pollen masses) to the stigma of another plant of the same species.

The methods they employ are so complex that it is *impossible* for them to cross—pollinate between species.

This keeps the plants true to type.

Only *mankind* has been able to cross-pollinate these beautiful flowers, in order to produce 'hybrids' purely for his own benefit.

The 'baby' mentioned earlier is, in fact, a landing platform for insects in the tiger orchid of Guatemala, *ONTONTOGLOSSUM GRANDE* . The illusion however, is very much in the eye of the beholder. While *some* people fancy they see a *'baby'*, others swear it is *'Santa Claus'!*

To the insect, however, this platform resembles a nectar-bearing flower. In fact, the flower offers *no* such reward! Once the insect *lands* upon the *platform*, however, the pollinia is released, ensuring fertilization.

Oddly enough, the insects never seem to *learn* by their mistakes, which surely proves that in *this* case at *least*, the *plant* is a good deal smarter than the *insect!*

The ghost orchid, *EPIPOGIUM APHYLLUM* is so called because of the ghost-like flowers of the plant, combined with the translucent appearance of the stem. This is due purely to the plant's lack of chlorophyll (the green colouring in plants).

This sickly appearance is due to the fact that the ghost orchid is a *saprophyte*. It attaches itself on to the roots of a 'host' plant and draws *sap* from it. This means that it gets all the nourishment it needs from it's 'host', making the presence of chlorophyll unnecessary.

The green chemical, *chlorophyll* is the agent which assists in photosynthesis, from which a plant gets much of it's energy. The Ghost Orchid occurs naturally from northern Europe to the Himalayas, and has also been recorded in the British Isles.

The 'flying duck' orchid of Australia is, perhaps, one of the strangest of *all* orchids, even though they live in a *land* of unique flora and fauna. Inhabitants of Australasia includes the *aborigine*, or native species of mankind, known as Australoid.

These are distinct from the *other* three races of mankind. the *Mongoloid*, which include the *Chinese, Japanese, Native Americans, Eskimos* and *Polynesians,* the *Negroid*, which include the *Africans* and

West Indians, and the *Caucasoids,* which include the *Europeans* and *Indians.*

The 'flying Duck' orchid (pictured p94) not only *resembles* a duck taking off, but even *flicks it's head* when an *insect* lands upon it.

By this method, the flower tosses the unsuspecting creature into a 'cup' formed by petals, so that it carries away the pollinia to another plant of the same species, after it escapes.

Once again, these flies never appear to learn from their experience!

Also in Australia is the 'bearded Orchid', *CALACHILUS ROBERTSONII* , which, to us mere humans, may resemble a *hippy* or a *bearded hillbilly*, although the plant *itself* has it's *own* reasons for it's strange appearance. The glossy hairs of the 'beard' *actually* mimic a hairy caterpillar which is found in the district. This caterpillar *also* happens to be the prey of an Australian species of *wasp.*

As the wasp tries to attack the 'caterpillar', it picks up the pollinia in readiness for it's next 'attack, during which it transfers the pollinia to the next flower!

In the flowers of the *MASDEVELLIA* orchids of *Peru*, many people see a *hooded gnome* lurking. When viewed from a *distance* however, the general outline strongly resembles that of a *hummingbird*, which happens to be the very creature which *pollinates* it!

When the male hummingbird tries to go though an act of *courtship* with this flower, (which he mistakes for a female), he doesn't fertilize a *female hummingbird* as he *believes,* but instead he fertilizes the *flower!*

Some *British* wild orchids are well up in the league of mimicry too. These include the *fly orchid*, which, when in bloom, looks for all the world as though several *flies* had settled upon the stem.

The *bee orchid* (pictured p94) and *spider orchid* also do good impressions of those particular insects. Please remember though, that if you are lucky enough to come across one of these exquisite plants during the course of a country walk, be content with taking photographs, or making sketches. They are rapidly disappearing from the wild, and are very unlikely to survive in the *garden*, for reasons mentioned earlier.

For all the natural talent of our native *British* orchids however the top award for mimicry must surely go to the wasp orchid *OPHRYS SPECULUM* (pictured p94), of the Mediterranean. Not only does this plant give an almost perfect impression of a *female wasp* found in those parts, but it also gives off the perfect *odour*, which attracts the, male wasp of the same species!

The *male wasp* can pick up this scent from an incredible distance of *FIVE MILES AWAY!*

When the intrepid suitor attempts to *copulate* with the imitation female, he again, picks up the pollinia, ready to transport it to another plant, which is ready and eager to attract his amorous desires!

So you see, insects, birds, animals and mankind *himself* often make mistakes.

Plants, however, with their vast experience of over two thousand million years, rarely do!

Orchids, which have, perhaps fired the imagination of Mankind more than any *other* group of plants, is also the largest group of flowering plants on Earth. They account for an estimated 35,000 species, one seventh, in fact, of *ALL* flowering plants.

They range from those with flowers as small as a pinhead as in the tiny Venezuelan orchid, *PLATESTELE ORNATA*, to the gorgeous *CATTLEYAS* of the South American tropics.

They are also regarded as the most *advanced* of all the flowering plants. It isn't really surprising then, that they have developed so many forms and ingenious mechanisms for the purposes of survival and perpetuation of the species.

Orchids have adapted themselves to live in *terra firma,* in conditions ranging from desert to marshland, upon the *roots of other plants* as *saprophytes*, and even on top of the highest trees in the Amazon rain forests, to enable them to get their fair share of the light.

They mimic *other* forms of life – butterflies to donkeys – yes, *DONKEYS!* Yet the one that baffled scientists for many years was a lovely white orchid from Madagascar, *ANGRECAECUM SESQUPEDALE.* This orchid has a 12- inch spur at the back of the flower, and as there was just a small sip of watery nectar at the end of

'Flying Duck' Orchid

Bee Orchid

Wasp Orchid

the spur, 19th century scientists couldn't understand what form of life could possible hope to get at the nectar!

They scoffed when Charles Darwin predicted that 'some huge moth with a proboscis a foot long' was responsible for the flower's pollination. Forty years later however, a night-flying moth with a 12-inch tongue was discovered on the island. It is the *only* creature on earth which is capable of pollinating this particular orchid! If this species of moth should become extinct, *so too would the orchid*!

One mystery however, *remains* about the plants we have discussed so far, and in particular those which mimic *other* forms of life.

If plants can't *see, hear* or *smell*, how can they *possibly* imitate the shapes and the scents of other living things, adapting themselves as they do, to appear to be like the forms of life which pollinate them? This will be discussed more fully in chapter eleven.

Of course, not *all* plants are pollinated by insects and birds. Some are wind-pollinated, in which case, the flowers do not *need* to be conspicuous, and indeed, many people don't even realise that *ALL* trees have flowers of *some* form or other, unless these flowers take the forms of catkins or really attractive blossoms such as those on flowering cherries.

OTHER PLANTS ARE POLLINATED BY *WATER*, BUT THEY STILL RELY ON BIRDS AND ANIMALS TO SPREAD THEIR SEEDS FAR AND WIDE.

TO THIS END, NATURE HAS DEVISED SOME PRETTY INTRIGUING FRIENDSHIPS BETWEEN THE PLANT AND THE ANIMAL KINGDOM ...

Chapter Ten

HELPING HANDS

There is *much* that man doesn't understand about nature and the world around him. This is largely due to the fact he believes everything is put upon this earth solely to suit *his* needs. This is certainly *not true*.

Everything exists upon this Garden Earth as a part of some supreme pattern, and once we can conquer the basic selfishness inherent in us all, then we may get somewhere near to understanding our brothers and sisters in the natural world.

Man is undoubtedly the most advanced form of life in the *Animal* Kingdom, whilst the orchids seems to command the same status in the *Plant* Kingdom. The main *difference* is that orchids do not try to *meddle* with nature in the way that *makind* does!

We all get annoyed when the birds eat the peas from our gardens, or the berries from our fruit and ornamental shrubs. We positively *seethe* when wasps attack our fruit trees, yet if only we would stop to *think,* they have as much right to live as *we* do.

They don't understand the time we spend in tending to our plants, or indeed, how much *money* we spend, simply because these values don't *exist* in nature.

Time *itself* is contrived by mankind, even though it is based on natural laws.

Money isn't any use to *any* of the earth's creatures except man, and he has become obsessed by its 'purchasing' power.

Everything in nature has been designed to be enjoyed by *ALL* living things. Indeed, it is *WE* who are the mugs, spending hard-earned cash on plants and materials which have already been *given* to us by nature!

By nature's law, no plant, no shrub, no tree, nor any piece of land should be 'owned' by any *one individual*.

The *entire earth* is our natural inheritance, but because we have chosen to divide this inheritance according to our social and financial positions, we cannot expect the rest of earth's creatures to fall in line with our dubious social structure.

It is true that many animals and birds 'stake out' their own territory, keeping creatures of their own kind at bay, but this is usually done simply to protect their ground from possible predators, and not simply by the greedy concept of 'ownership'.

Every living thing has a right to a stable existence.

Can you imagine the public outrage, if a group of people blew up a block of flats whilst the residents were still at home, just so that they could built their own house upon the site?

That is *exactly* what we are doing when we fell, and uproot a tree, so that we may claim the land for ourselves.

That tree was home to hundreds of birds, squirrels, and other small creatures, and millions of insects.

What right have we to evict millions of creatures, purely for our own greed?

We feel deeply upset when the birds pick the buds off our primulas and crocuses. While some of this activity may be due, as I said earlier, to brain damage through lead and carbon monoxide poisoning , it is *also* possible that our feathered friends may actually be doing the plants a *service*!

In commerce, flower buds are removed from plants to encourage the rootstock to increase. The practice of preventing the plants from reproducing sexually by removing the flowers encourage them to reproduce *vegetatively* -by means of the roots.

Likewise, when a gardener transplants a herbaceous plant, it is a good idea to remove the *flowers,* so that the energy is redirected into producing a good *root system* for anchorage and feeding purposes.

It is doubtful that the birds actually *realise* they are doing the plant a service, but it is worth noting that when the plant has established a nice plump *colony,* the birds seem to leave the plants alone. It is very rare indeed to find flowers emasculated in this way in the *wild,* where plants have grown naturally from seed and matured in situ.

Generally speaking, *transplanted* plants are more prone to attack from birds.

As far as the *berries on the trees* are concerned, the simple fact that they taste *good* to the birds is an effort by the plant to *encourage* our feathered friends to eat the fruits! They eat the *whole* berry, *seed and all,* only to release the seed in their droppings, perhaps several miles away.

The young seedlings get off to an admirable start, complete with it's own supply of humus material!

Man has only *recently* caught up with nature in the production *of pelleted seeds!*

On the *other* hand, when *we* eat fruit, we throw away the core, which contains the seeds.

Social behaviour dictates that we throw the core into a *litter bin.* In *this* case, maybe flouting the litter laws by throwing it to the *ground* is a *good thing!*

Indeed, throwing any biodegradable material onto the ground is a help to nature. Problems for the natural world arise only when we leave *non-*biodegradable litter such as *metal cans* and *plastics* laying around. But then, these are *man-made* objects!

Other seeds attach themselves to the *fur of passing animals,* so that they eventually get rubbed off, when the animal *scratches itself,* some distance away.

These methods help the plant to distribute the species over a wide area.

The classic example of animals helping plants is, of

course, in the case of the squirrel. Although recent studies prove that before a squirrel buries an acorn in the ground, it bites off the growing tip to *prevent* it from growing. Many are buried intact however, and whilst it has also proved a fallacy that squirrel forgets where he buried the acorns, the odd few *DO* escape his notice through other factors. and they grow on to make new trees.

The oak tree itself has *another* trick up it's sleeve for ensuring continuity of it's species. If an acorn drops at the foot of an aged 'mother' tree, it germinates, and taps its young root into the root of the 'mother' tree. This way, it lives off its parent's sap until that parent tree dies! The reason for this is that when a sapling starts growing under another tree, it would normally get starved of nutrients and sunlight.

This 'suckling' of the young oak ensures that it replaces it's mother when she finally dies!

Parasites, saprophytes and epiphytes (those that live in humus on the branches of trees) all live on 'host' plants. Unlike *human* parasites however, they all have a very necessary place in nature's plan.

Fungi and lichens live on dead decaying vegetation This way, they act, together with the animal kingdom's scavengers such as vultures and hyenas, as nature's very own 'refuse disposal units'.

Without *these,* and all the myriads of insects and bacteria, we would all be walking knee-deep in litter.

A bit like Britain's big cities in fact!

The main difference is that nature's methods of 'waste disposal' are far more efficient! Only man-made products such as tin cans, glass, plastic bottles and bags, and rubber tyres cause a problem for nature, and very often the effects are *lethal.*

There have been many cases of small animals and birds suffering from cuts caused by broken glass and plastic, as well as suffocation from plastic bags.

That great Christmas favourite, the *mistletoe* is a *saprophyte.* It lives off the *sap* of a tree, rather than the actual *tissues,* as does a *parasite.*

The berries when ripe, are sticky. Birds find these very attractive to eat, but the seeds stick to their beaks, making things uncomfortable for then. When the bird lands on another *tree,* they rub their beaks on the bark to get rid of the sticky stuff, leaving the seeds in crevices in the tree, where they germinate and grow.

Many equatorial orchids are *epiphytic.* In *other* words, they live on the branches of trees, but instead of tapping the *sap of the host* as do the *saprophytes,* they receive their nourishment from deposits of *humus,* formed by leaves and animal droppings, which have become wedged in cracks and crevasses.

The stag's horn fern *platycerium spp.,* and the Christmas cactus, *zygocactus truncatus* also live in the way, and the reasons for this lifestyle are twofold.

Firstly, it allows them to get nearer to the life-giving sunlight, as there is not much light deep down at the bottom of a rain forest! Secondly, it makes the flowers more conspicuous to high-flying insects, birds and bats, all of which play a part in the fertilization of the flowers, and the distribution of the seeds.

Many orchids are so complex in the flower arrangements that only *one* type of insect, bird or bat can possibly pollinate them.

As we have said before about *other* plants, this lessens the chances of cross-pollination of related species, thus keeping one particular species true to type. *Otherwise,* the earth would be full of *hybrid* plants with no *true species.*

If *this* were allowed to happen, there would eventually only be *ONE* common hybrid of each species!

There are, of course, *other* safeguards against cross-pollination of both *related* and *non*-related species.

Some plants have different *chromosome counts,* so that the plants involved are genetically incompatible. Others produce pollen grains of various size, which simply will not react to the stigmas of other species or sub-species.

Mankind uses *many* methods to try to break this natural law. One is by means of drugs (to double chromosome counts). Another is by shortening the stigma of the seed-bearer (so that a small pollen grain can grow sufficiently down the style to the ovaries).

Yet *another* way is simply by bringing together related plants from different parts of the world.

Primulas for example, are considered very 'promiscuous' by our way of thinking, and will cross-breed with their close cousins readily. The fact is, of course, that they normally live *miles* apart, either on a different continent, or in the same country, but in different locations. Normally, there is very little chance that they will breed together. Again, Mankind has upset the balance! Growing together in the same garden or greenhouse, it is difficult to keep the species true to type !

Gardeners get *annoyed* about this. All I can say is, - it's their own fault, - or at least, the fault of the great plant hunters who brought them together in the *first* place!

There is little doubt that in the case of plant breeding, Mankind has, himself, lent nature a 'helping hand' by assisting evolution by means of selective breeding, or by vegetative propagation, although in *many* cases he has also produced monstrosities which would *never* survive in nature.

It is also likely that he is actually causing the *extinction* of many true species of plants, by hybridizing them out of existence.

For example, the Spanish bluebell, being a much more robust species than it's British counterpart, has escaped from gardens, crossed with native bluebells in the woods, leaving many woods with only Spanish types, and their hybrids. The sad fact is that the British bluebell is far daintier, and unlike it's Spanish cousin, is heavily scented.

There is, though, evidence that nature will actually *FOLLOW* Mankind's lead by producing plants *naturally* which have already been bred or developed by Man.

Often, in an ornamental garden, where foliage plants have been used, a wild plant will suddenly start producing ornamental leaves, as if a conscious effort has been made by the plant to compete with it's more ornamental companions!

I have found a wild plum that suddenly started sporting variegated leaves, after two ornamental shrubs had been planted either side of it.

I have even *looked* at a plant and *imagined* what it would look like in a different colour. As if by magic, the following season, one of those plants have produced flowers of the colour I had imagined!

Is it possible then, that plants may even know what we are *THINKING*? More about that in the *next* chapter.

Because of their enquiring nature, and their ability to cover long distances in a short space of time, birds are the plants' natural allies when it comes to distributing seeds. Amazingly, they even take and distribute *plant cuttings*!

The common yellow stonecrop, *SEDUM ACRE*, has a pleasant, though *bitter* taste. It often grows upon walls and has a 'peppery' taste. Hence it's British country name of 'wall pepper'.

Birds find the succulent little leaves quite irresistible. They peck them off for their moisture. However, when they discover it's 'peppery' taste, they toss it out of their beaks, scattering it all over the ground. There, the tiny pieces of leaf take root, distributing the plant over a wider area!

Even the humble *bacteria* make a wonderful contribution to the welfare of plants. *Without* them, decaying vegetation would not be broken into the chemical nutrients which are essential for healthy plant growth.

IPERRII 93

Sparrow

Indeed, some bacteria are *themselves* classified as plants, so here we have just one example of plants working together for the *common good!*

In the *legumes*, (clovers, peas, lupins, etc.,) the plants *themselves* form swollen nodules at the root-ends with the specific purpose of accommodating bacteria which are necessary for the healthy growth of the plant.

The *plant* provides a *home* for the *bacteria*, whilst the *bacteria* provides *food* for the *plant*, by breaking down nutrients which are in the soil.

If you cannot grow lupins successfully in *your* garden, try planting some *clover* in the ground the year before planting the lupins and see the difference! You see, the clover *encourages* the bacteria to grow, and the following year, the bacteria will assist your *lupin* plants to grow well!

There are *many* examples of plant associations that the gardener would do well to remember.

Wood anemones and wood sorrel seem to grow better in the company of bluebells and primroses.

The Scots primrose, *primula Scotica*, only gives of it's best when planted with certain dwarf grasses or the pearlwort, *sagina procumbens*. In *this* case, it is thought that the roots of the grasses or pearlwort prevent the tiny primula roots from drying out.

In the Scottish Highlands, the Scots primrose grows *only* in damp grassy meadows and hillocks. It cannot grow succesfully without that kind of company!

Fungi are very *particular* as to the company they keep. For instance, the *fly agaric* will only grow on the decaying leaves of *birches*. Any attempt to grow them anywhere else will inevitably end in failure.

In fact, by trying to *understand* plants, we get much nearer to understanding the whole of life's pattern, and *this garden earth*.

PRIMROSE

Bacteria producing the elements necessary for *plant growth*. The *plants* producing *food* for the *animals*. The *animals* carrying the *seeds* of the plants, to grow on the *elements* produced by the *bacteria*.

So it goes on. This cycle is repeated without fail, over and over again, in many complex forms.

There are so many permutations and complexities *within* the cycle, that it would take several volumes to go into it in detail.

For the purpose of the book then, we'll be content with the examples we have already discussed.

SO FAR, WE HAVE COVERED THE MANY *PHYSICAL* ASPECTS OF PLANT LIFE. WHAT, THOUGH, OF THEIR *DRIVE*, THEIR *FEELINGS*, THEIR *CHARACTER?*

DO PLANTS HAVE *EMOTIONS* THAT *WE* CAN UNDERSTAND?

THERE IS GROWING EVIDENCE THAT THEY *DO, INDEED!*

Chapter Eleven:

THE 'EMOTIONS' OF PLANTS

Before I prune any tree or shrub in my garden, I give them two weeks' notice of my intentions, so that they can withdraw energy and prepare themselves for the shock.

I also warn my plants before I split them up for propagation and before I transplant them.

Does this seem *stupid* to you?

Is it?

Let us now look a little deeper into the 'psychology' of plants, as far as we are able to understand it.

Who knows, in the future, the USA, who already have *animal* psychologists, might come up with the idea of *plant* psychologisits.

But remember - you read it here first!

We have already established that plants react positively to outside stimuli, in a similar way to us. In fact, they seem to have an even *higher* degree of sensitivity to *certain* things, such as *light, gravity* and the *earth's rotation*.

We have *also* shown that plants are very much aware of the hazards around them,, and are capable of *dealing* with them. This *alone* must surely suggest that plants have some power of *reason*.

Recent experiments show that the feelings of plants may go far *beyond* this, and even possibly beyond our *own* delicate emotional structures, to the mysterious realms of *telepathy!*

Many old gardeners will tell you that they actually *talk* to their plants. Indeed, *Prince Charles* has gone on record as saying much the same thing. *I also* talk to my plants, and often refer to seedlings in a tray as 'my babies'.

There are many stories of ordinary folk who tend their plants with loving care, being rewarded with wonderful flowers and luscious fruits. They appear to have more success than their more 'down to earth' friends, who go 'by the book'.

Why should this be?

Can plants actually *HEAR* the kind words spoken to them? Are they capable of understanding *all human languages?* It is more likely that they can either actually feel the emotional 'vibrations' of people, or they can read their minds!

It is certainly true that plants appear to respond to *emotional* atmospheres, as well as to *physical* atmospheres. It has been noted that house plants seem to thrive better in a home where the family are *happy*, or when they live a peaceful existence in the care of elderly people.

On the *other* hand, a household which is full of rows and petty arguments *never* seem capable of nurturing really healthy plants.

Plants *also* appear to respond to *threats* and *ultimatums*! Many reports have been published in which people have grown fed up with a plant which refuses to flower. The grower has threatened to throw it away. The result in many cases is that the plant has promptly started to flower!

One year, I sowed some lawn seed late in the season, merely because it was available. Being a professional gardener, I didn't really expect any results as I was 'going against the book'. I wasn't in the least surprised then, when a couple of months later, the ground was still bare. I explained to my wife Shirley that, being the beginning of December, it was unlikely that seed would germinate *at all*.

Undeterred however, out went Shirley to the barren patch threatening them, 'if you grass seeds don't start growing *soon*, I'm coming out here and I'm *digging you all up*!' Amazingly, just *ONE WEEK LATER*, there were tiny blades of grass coming through. By the following summer we had a lush lawn! That little experience taught me a lot, and yet I thought *I* was the expert!

In 1969, in the city of New York, private investigator and inventor of the polygraph, *Cleve Backster* was about to water his philodendron plants.

The thought suddenly occurred to him that a *polygraph*, or 'lie detector' in the office might possibly record the time it takes for the water to travel from the roots of the plant to the upper leaves.

With this in mind, he promptly hooked the device up to the plant. To Cleve's utter amazement, the machine recorded an immediate response from the plant which, had it been hooked to a *human being*, would have been interpreted as a sense of *joy*!

Cleve Backster

Even *more* amazing was the fact that this joyous response was recorded PRIOR TO THE WATER BEING ADMINISTERED, SUGGESTING SOME FORM OF ANTICIPATION ON THE PART OF THE PLANT. IN OTHER WORDS, THE PLANT KNEW IT was GOING TO BE WATERED!

Wondering whether the plant was actually capable of *reading his mind*, Backster then thought about testing the plant for signs of *pain* by lighting a match and burning a leaf.

THE MACHINE RECORDED A STRONG SENSE OF FEAR, WHICH SENT THE RECORDING PEN BOUNCING RIGHT OFF THE TOP OF THE CHART AT THE SPLIT SECOND THAT BACKSTER CONCEIVED AN IMAGE IN HIS MIND OF BURNING THE LEAF WITH A MATCH!

Since those early experiments, Backster has collected quite a file of data on the emotions and pleasures of plants.

He has discovered that plants show a great deal of apprehension when a *dog* passes by. If a plant is attacked, in a roomful of people, neighbouring plants showed distinct signs of nervousness when the attacker approached *them,* but remained quite calm when anybody *else* approached them! This suggests that plants can recognise a potential enemy.

Just imagine what a *tree* feels like, when a gang of men approaches it with a *chain saw*!

If you feel a little *sceptical* about Backster's claims, then think on this: *The Mary Reynolds Babcock Foundation of America* were so *impressed* with his work that have donated *$10,000* to help in his research!

Backster, however, isn't the *only* one to have recorded the reactions of plants to emotional stress. A team of scientists in Russia have recorded sharp reactions to *pain*, registered by a *tomato plant* when it was cut.

They have even recorded, with the help of highly sensitive equipment, the screams of a *carrot* as it was pulled out of the ground. A *tree* has *also* been recorded sceaming in terror as an *axe* struck it's trunk. It is believed that *some* animals, notably *dogs*, can actually *hear* these screams.

I have noticed *myself* that, if a dog is nearby when a tree is being cut down, it cowers in fright and runs away with it's tail between it's legs. It is as though it is trying to escape from some ear-splitting noise, inaudible to human ears.

In 1989, British scientists acknowledged that trees *do* scream, after using a sonic device on trees which were being *felled*. It is quite probable then, that plants not only *FEEL* pain, but actually *respond* to it in the same way that *we* and the *animals* do. The only reason we don't *realise* this is that our ears simply aren't *sensitive* enough!

In 1968, I had reason to leave a trough of my beloved primulas with my sister, Eileen for a couple of weeks. They were perfectly *healthy* at the time, and, being hardy, they were left in the back garden, where they were watered as per my instructions. Upon my return however, the plants were looking decidedly sick.

Naturally, I was very *concerned* about this state of affairs. I couldn't put any blame on my *sister*, as she had followed my instructions to the letter.

I took hold of the yellowing leaves, muttering, 'what's the matter then, feeling a bit sick are you? Never mind, I'm back to look after you now.' My sister thought I was *mad!*

I had no time that night to administer any special *treatment*, and yet, the following morning, to my utter delight, the limp leaves had become 'turgid' again. Within a few days, they were bright green, and glowing with health! It was as though my plants had actually *missed* me whilst I had been away. If only I'd had *Backster's equipment* at that time!

An even *sadder* case occurred in 1967. My young wife Dorothy and I were extremely happy, with two little girls and our own house in Blackpool. I was working on the Blackpool Corporation parks department, and was designing the woodland garden mentioned in an earlier chapter.

Then, as now, primulas were my special *love* in the plant world. I was *particularly* delighted when I raised a double yellow seedling polyanthus. I promptly named *Dorothy*, after my wife.

In June of that year, my young wife died suddenly of a brain haemmhorrage. Naturally, what with the grief, and making arrangements for my two young daughters, it was *months* before I could attend the garden.

When I found the time and the inclination to inspect the garden, I discovered that all of my plants were still in good shape, except for the double polyanthus *DOROTHY*. She had *also* died, along with my darling wife. I have never been able to breed a double polyanthus quite so beautiful.

The big question of course, is *how* can plants possibly respond in this way? How can they manage to copy something they *apparently* cannot see nor smell, -at least, in any way that *WE* can understand?

From Backster's experiments, it seems likely that plants *CAN* see, hear and smell what is in *our* minds.

Is it possible then, that they can use the creatures *about* them, to enable them to 'see' , 'hear' and 'smell' all that is around them?

It may seem pretty far-fetched to us mere humans, but then so does everything *else* until we can study and understand them!

It is even possible that plants are a *much higher life-form* than animals. It could be that they are actually capable of *using* us and the

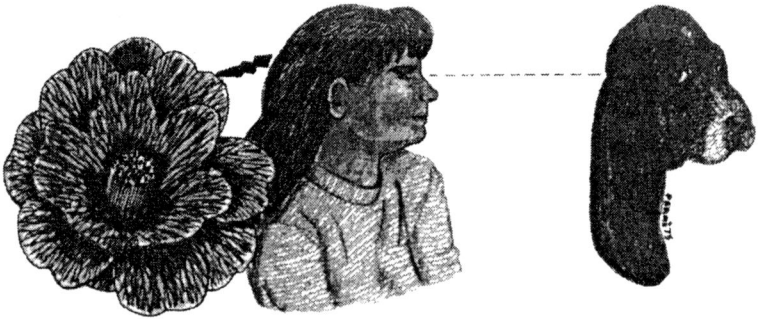

Do plants use our eys to 'see' things?

other animals for the senses that *we* possess, and *they* lack, *sight, hearing* and sense of *smell!*

After all, these senses are passed through our *minds*, which is something which we *still* do not fully understand.

If plants are capable of probing our minds as Backster's experiments appear to suggest, then they may well be able to make use of our *physical* senses too, through *telepathic powers!*

In 1978, after complex experiments, a team of Russian scientists, suggested not only that trees can *communicate with each other by means of telepathy*, but that they can do so at *great distances*. They suggested that they may even be capable of communicating in this way to plant life on *other planets!*

If this is so, is it not possible that the process could be *reversed*, and that some of the great ideas and inventions that have occurred during the course of civilisation have been picked up by trees on *other planets* from a higher intelligence than ourselves, beamed to trees on *earth*, and then picked up subconsciously by mankind on this planet?

Who knows?

It was discovered, however, in November, 2001, that plants do have very good, and surprisingly long, memories, and this research has added to the evidence that plants may be able to see, hear, smell, taste and see, even if, perhaps, in a different way to animals.

Professor Caroline Dean and a team of researchers discovered these secrets whilst unraveling the DNA blueprint of a plant for the first time. It appears that a particular gene enables plants to remember weather conditions that they have encountered over a period of weeks, months, and even years.

Depending upon the species, the plant stores the memories of cold weather, then it waits for a certain amount of time before it flowers. This could also account for genetic changes leading to new species and sub-species.

Dr Colin Nicholls, who was also on the research team at The John Innes Centre in Norwich. Has explained that the secret ability allowed plants to judge when it is a good time to bloom.

'It is a sort of memory,' He said at the time, 'and it is a very sophisticated system. It enables plants to make sure it doesn't flower at the wrong time.'

The team, which published its findings in the scientific journal *Cell*, has called the memory gene VRN2. This stands for vernalisation, an acceleration of flowering, following a cold period of three to eight weeks. At temperatures of 4 to 8 degrees Centigrade.

The experts say that there were three clear stages in a plant's seasonal cycle: The first was the time when the plant first knew it was experiencing winter, and the second phase was when it knew it had been through a cold period, and began growing again, ready to flower. In the final phase, the plant actually flowered.

The plant used was thale cress, a member of the mustard family. Because it is biologically simple, and grows quickly, with as many as eight generations in a year.

Dr. Nicholls also said that when they removed the memory gene from the plant, it acted as though it had no knowledge of seasonal changes.

They also discovered that plants have proteins that can detect light, as in phototropism, and they may even allow the plants to detect wavelengths beyond the range of the human eye!

Studies also discovered that if one tree is damaged by pests, those close to it suffer less. They believe that the first tree warns its neighbours, so that they can develop protection by emitting smells that the pests find repulsive.

Other studies showed that plants are able to 'taste' nutrients in the soil, and grow towards ares in the soil that are rich in the best nutrients, and also that plants also respond to sounds.

Incidentally, if all this has put you off eating fruit and veg, then remember that *animals* don't like being killed *either*! It is worth remembering that plants are the only living beings on this Earth which produce material *solely* for the purpose of being *eaten*! This is certainly true of *fruit and nuts*, even though the plants have an ulterior motive in distributing their seeds!

Plants even produce *nectar*, the *sole diet* of many insects and birds. This is consumed, not only without danger to the plants *themselves*, but for the specific purpose of *reproduction*!

Now *that's* what I call a clever system, and one which is peculiar to the plant kingdom. Plants also have a *digestive system* which is ingenious in it's simplicity, and which does not produce *waste products*, as does the digestive systems of *animals*!

ARE THE PLANTS SHOWING US A WAY OF LIVING WITHOUT THE NECESSITY OF KILLING ANY LIVING THING, PLANT OR ANIMAL?

If we try to understand the *purposes* and the *feelings* of plants, we come to realise that they are actually *living beings*, rather than simply 'things which grow from the ground'.

If we can understand *this*, we may begin to treat them with the respect they *deserve!*

Perhaps, if we could introduce this information into *educational systems*, we might be able to put a stop to vandalism, not only by the odd thoughtless *youth*, but also by our *town planners, building contractors, politicians*, and all those who are Hell-bent on mutilating and destroying This Garden Earth.

THIS PLANET BELONGS TO *ALL* LIVING THINGS, AND IS NOT SIMPLY A PLAYGROUND OR BATTLEFIELD FOR MANKIND'S SELFISH DESIRES.

WE *MUST* MAKE SURE THAT WE BEGIN TO UNDO ALL THE *HARM* WE HAVE DONE.

WILL WE FIGHT FOR OUR LIVES, -OR SWITCH THE LIFE SUPPORT SYSTEM OFF?

IT IS UP TO US ALL ...

THIS GARDEN EARTH

CONCLUSION

Throughout this book, I have tried to explain to you, the reader, how plant life first populated this Garden Earth over two thousand million years ago; how it struggled for existence upon a young planet which would be far too hostile for any other form of life.

We have gone through the 'Age of the Giants' and the Great Ice Age to the emergence of Mankind some three million years ago.

We have seen how man began his infant years as the 'caretaker' of the planet, working in harmony with nature.

Unfortunately for all life upon earth, this 'caretaker' became the 'plunderer' during his teenage years. As he became aware of his own self-importance, he became wracked with greed, plundering the earth's valuable resources and destroying plant life, which are the very 'lungs' of the earth. He went on to pollute the land, the waters and the atmosphere.

Throughout the ages, however, there have been human beings who have continued to work *with* nature.

These were the witch doctors, medicine men and wise men mentioned at the beginning of chapter four, and it is to these we must look for the healthy future of our planet.

Many *plant breeders* have worked with nature to provide our gardens with beautiful flowers, succulent fruits and tasty vegetables, and where this has been done by selective breeding and the propagation of natural 'sports', I am sure that this fits in with mankind's destiny as 'caretaker'.

When, however, he uses drugs, radiation and genetic engineering techniques to effect changes, then I have serious doubts!

I do believe that mankind *will* realise the folly of his ways before it's too late. Indeed, in the late eighties, people were *forced* to take conservation seriously with the 'official' discovery of a hole in the ozone layer.

Unfortunately, whilst many politicians appeared to become 'green' , they did very little of significance.

STILL, as we enter the new millennium, industry, commerce and economics take precedence over conservation!

Hopefully, as Mankind travels deeper into the final frontier of space, he will appreciate more, the marvels of nature, and his insignificance in the greater plan of things.

He may well discover that our neighbouring planets, Venus and Mars, were once inhabited by intelligent beings such as ourselves, and that it was through *their* folly that the planets of the solar system became devoid of life!

Scientists now *know* that Mars has a thin atmosphere, made up mainly of carbon dioxide, and that it's red dust-covered surface is riddled with craters, similar to those on the Moon.

Is it not possible that at one time, Mars was *inhabited* much as the Earth is today, and that some great catastrophe, - perhaps even a *nuclear holocaust*, were responsible for the barren planet we observe today?

The nuclear war theory seems even *more* likely when you consider the craters on the surface, and mysterious glass marble—like spheres, which occur all over the planets' surface.

This phenomenon could *only* have occurred during sudden intense heat such as nuclear explosion!

Whilst Mars is *smaller* than the Earth, with a very thin atmosphere, *Venus* is virtually the Earth's twin, being similar in size, with a year of 2243/4 Earth days, spinning on it's axis once every 243 Earth days. There, however, the similarity ends.

The surface of Venus is far *too hot* to contain life as we know it. It also has a very dense atmosphere of carbon dioxide, with traces of gases, including sulphur dioxide and carbon monoxide, -exactly the conditions that would occur on earth with a prolonged 'greenhouse effect' due to pollution and the destruction of the ozone layer! COULD IT BE THAT THE INTENSELY HOT, ROCK-STREWN SURFACE OF VENUS IS AN INDICATION OF WHAT THE EARTH MIGHT BE LIKE IN PERHAPS TWO HUNDRED YEARS IF WE DON'T MAKE GOOD THE MISTAKES WE'VE MADE IN THE PAST?

ONLY WHEN MAN SETS FOOT ON THE PLANET'S SURFACE, PROTECTED BY HEAT-RESISTANT SUITS AND A GOOD SUPPLY OF OXYGEN, WILL WE KNOW FOR SURE!

We may think of programmes such as *Star Trek* as pure fantasy. It is however, quite possible for mankind to re-establish Venus as a life-supporting planet, merely by 'seeding' the surface with heat-resistant plants from earth, so that those plants can begin the process of converting all that carbon Dioxide into oxygen, in readiness for mankind and the animals to re-colonise it.

'Operation Genesis One' (O.G.O.) would certainly eleviate the pressures we put upon This Garden Earth by population growth. It might also make us appreciate fully the importance of the plant life upon our *home* planet!

The question now is whether *ALL* dominant life-forms with intelligence such as ours, have set themselves upon a crash-course against nature. The answer is probably *not!*

Firstly, let us assume that dominant life-forms which exist upon planets *OUTSIDE* the solar system are *humanoid* (similar in appearance to ourselves).

I *personally* believe that intelligent life forms which are living upon a remote planet will be making contact with us very soon. Possibly by the year 2010AD., and *probably* via satellite television, and through the internet.

The reason why I believe this is that our television broadcasting system, together with the internet, is becoming so sophisticated and widespread via orbiting satellites, that it would make sense for alien beings to make their presence known to as many people as possible.

They could contact people of all nationalities at the same time by taking over as many different channels and websites as possible.

This would make far more sense than for them to cause alarm and panic by simply landing their spacecraft in cities around the earth, as was a popular conception in all those 1950s Science fiction films!

This way, they would be less of a potential *threat* to the people of earth, and therefore less vulnerable to hostilities from political and military factions.

It would *also* give them the opportunity to prove to us that they are very similar to ourselves.

They would also be able to 'educate' us in the *care* of our planet. Let's face it, if they were advanced enough to travel *great distances in space*, then surely they would have come to terms with the delicate balance of their *own planet?*

You may be sure that by the time they *do* make contact with us, they will be well acquainted with our customs and our languages.

This way, they will be able to communicate easily with any nation on earth in their own language.

Indeed, *some* commentators have suggested that world leaders are *already* aware of the forthcoming contact by 'other world civilizations.'

This is why great strides have been made to unite the peoples of the Earth during the late eighties and nineties, in time for the dawning of the new millennium.

Witness perestroika and glasnost, which led to the break-up the USSR, the coming together of the European community, the reforms in Afghanistan and Poland, the demolition of the Berlin Wall, the peace efforts in the middle east, and the peace deal in Ireland.

Personally, I believe many more reforms will take place, both politically and environmentally, before the 'contact' year of 2010. Once contact has been *made*, This Garden Earth will be heading for what the hippies of the sixties called *'The Age of Aquarius'*, where 'love and peace will guide the planet'. Not simply between the *human* races of the earth, but between *all* living creatures, the earth, planets, and the universe as a whole.

Why then, you may ask, have not the ordinary people of the earth been *told* about *contact year*?

The answer is simple .

Would *YOU* believe the politicians, -even if they united to make a common statement?

Would *YOU* believe the scientists?

Would you believe *ME?*

Of *course* not!

Ordinary people need *proof,* and what better way than for our friends from other planets to broadcast *directly to us?*

Telecommunications probably represents the greatest power ever produced by mankind.

It breaks down the barriers between countries and races which have been built up over the centuries by politicians and the military.

Satellite TV and the internet have opened up the world to *everyone*. We can now *SEE* what conditions are like elsewhere on earth, without having to rely on propaganda put out by self-interested parties.

IN SHORT, IT IS MAKING US REALISE THAT WE ARE *ALL* INHABITANTS OF *ONE EARTH*, RATHER THAN SIMPLY A MEMBER OF ANY PARTICULAR COUNTRY.

AT LAST MANKIND IS BEGINNING TO GROW UP, AND SHAKING OFF HIS 'TRIBAL' INSTINCTS!

I believe that our friends from other planets will be able to take our education much further, and teach us how to live in harmony with all living things

When this happens, the human race will move out of his 'teenage years' finally growing into 'adulthood'. He will, of course, have to serve a probationary period of 'community service' in order to put right the damage he did in his youth!

HOPEFULLY, AS MAN *DISCARDS* HIS TRIBAL INSTINCTS, HE WILL PUT BEHIND HIM *FOREVER* THE OLD TRADITIONS THAT HAVE CAUSED WARS, POLLUTION AND THE RAPE OF THE EARTH.

THESE TRADITIONS INCLUDE *PATRIOTISM* AND *RELIGION*, FOR HE WILL LEARN NOT ONLY THAT WE ARE *ALL* INHABITANTS OF *THIS GARDEN EARTH,* BUT THAT GOD IS *GREEN.*

FOR WITHOUT PLANTS, ALL LIFE ON EARTH WOULD CEASE TO EXIST!

Further Reading

*If you want to know the full extent of mankind's damage to this planet, a follow-up to *This Garden Earth* will soon be available from this publisher.

Titled *Vandals in the Garden*, it is an anthology of mankind's destruction.

*Also in preparation is *We the Aliens*, which puts forward some astounding theories on mankind's origins.

© Pete Perry 2005